METHODS *of* USING

the

C L U B

for

SELF–DEFENSE

and

EXERCISE

in

NINETEENTH CENTURY GERMANY.

BY

BEN MILLER

HOLLY-WOOD,
Hudson Society Press.

Anno MM. XXII.

Cover art and book design by Bronwyn Frazier-Miller. Printed in the United States of America and the United Kingdom.

DISCLAIMER: The author, publisher, creators, and distributors of this book are not responsible, in any way whatsoever, for any loss, damage, injury, or any other adverse consequences that may result from the study, practice, or improper use made by anyone of the information or techniques contained in this book. All use of the information contained in this book must be made in accordance with what is permitted by law, and any damage liable to be caused as a result thereof will be the exclusive responsibility of the user. Many of the techniques described herein could lead to serious injury if not practiced under the guidance and training of a qualified instructor using appropriate safety equipment. This book is not a substitute for formal training. It is the sole responsibility of every person planning to train in the techniques described in this book to consult with a licensed physician before beginning.

Publisher's Cataloging-in-Publication data

Miller, Ben.

   Method of Using the Club for Self-Defense and Exercise in Nineteenth Century Germany / Ben Miller.

   pages cm.

Paperback: ISBN 978-0-9990567-6-9

   1. Fencing. 2. Dueling. 3. Swordplay. 4. Martial arts—History—19th century. 5. Germany— History. I. Miller, Ben. II. Title.

FIRST EDITION

10 9 8 7 6 5 4 3 2 1

Dedicated to my grandfather,
David Paul Miller, Sr. (1917-2011)

CONTENTS

ACKNOWLEDGMENTS

For their help in preparing this work for publication, I would like to thank the following individuals:

My wife, Bronwyn Frazier-Miller, for her consummate work in restoring numerous antique images reproduced in this book, for her cover design, for her feedback regarding both text and images, and for her ever-steadfast love and support.

My fencing masters, Maestro Ramón Martínez and Maestro Jeannette Acosta-Martínez, for their invaluable guidance, insight, and encouragement, for their suggestions regarding portions of the manuscript, and for their continued mentorship on and off the *salle* floor.

A huge thank you to Tobias Zimmermann, for his generous assistance with the English translation of Rothstein's *Die Keulenführung als Gymnastische Uebung,* which contains antiquated and often challenging German. Tobias also provided invaluable insight into some of the nuances of 19th century German history and fencing terminology, much of which has been included here in the modern footnotes to Rothstein's text, and for which I am greatly indebted.

David Mastro, for his insight and suggestions into the use of the club and related mythological motifs by nineteenth century European strongmen, for his assistance in sourcing historical images for the introduction, and for his feedback regarding the manuscript.

Maestro Paul Macdonald, for his insight into Hans Talhoffer's club, or *kolben*.

Robert Brooks, for reviewing portions of the introduction, and for his suggestions and insight into medieval German fencing history.

Carl Massaro and Mike Smith, for their feedback, and review of portions of the manuscript.

Maxime Chouinard, Oliver Janseps, and Michael Chidester, for their help in sourcing and determining copyright status of historical images.

Michael Smallridge and Peter Bates for assistance in finding information relating to the medieval Brabant Chronicle.

My parents, David and Pam Miller, as well as Jack and Pam Frazier, for their generous support throughout the years.

Ben Miller
Hollywood, California
October 2022

Now the club, the mace, and the morning-star recede into the background as weapons, and the age in which firearms technology has made such admirable advances relegates these oldest weapons of mankind to the junk room. Only in the museums of our great cities do clubs still parade as remnants of a great age, and we stand pondering before these ancient implements which, as a result of their use in training as individual weapons, also have a rich and certainly no less interesting history to show than the magnificent, artistically crafted swords. But, if one believes that the club has completely fallen out of use in the present, one is mistaken...

- H. Wortmann, Leipzig, 1885

Detail from dish (piatto), Italian, ca. 1510. The story of Hercules: the gods called upon Hercules to help them defend Olympus against the attack of the Giants, sons of Uranus and Gaea. Metropolitan Museum of Art, Accession Number: 1975.1.1036.

I.

INTRODUCTION

It may come as a surprise to some modern readers that, during the mid-nineteenth century, one could walk into a prominent Royal Berlin gymnasium, pay tuition, and take a class in the European art and science of how to fence with a long, heavy, two-handed club, for the purpose of both self-defense and the cultivation of mind, body, and spirit.

This seems to fly in the face of common knowledge. When the average person thinks of fencing as it was practiced during the nineteenth century, they are apt to assume that the only fencing weapons in use during that period consisted of the foil, épée (dueling sword), and sabre. Indeed, those were the weapons *de rigueur* in common use during the era —the staple curriculum of fencing academies, and the main feature of public contests and exhibitions, throughout both Europe and the Americas. However, during the same period, fencing theory was applied to a diverse variety of other weapons, both modern and ancient, both long and short, both one-handed and two-handed. These included weapons for which instruction was in practical demand at the time, such as the bayonet, broadsword, bowie knife, cane, lance, scythe, and spear. Additionally, the use of antiquated weapons—whose period of popularity had long since passed—was still remembered and preserved in a limited number of *salles des armes* and military academies.[1] These included weapons such as the rapier, dagger, cloak, quarterstaff, flail, as well as others. Additionally, the use of some medieval-era weapons—which was assumed to be extinct—was reconstructed and revived by fencing masters who had a keen interest in the fencing literature of the past.[2]

The club, however, hails from an even earlier epoch—from the Neolithic period (and probably earlier), when it was associated with the most primitive and savage mode of fighting.[3] This fact was not lost on fencing masters of the nineteenth century, who often commenced their histories of fencing by mentioning the club as the first or "original" primeval weapon. For instance, in 1877, Colonel Thomas Hoyer Monstery, a famous Danish-American duelist and fencing master, wrote in his treatise on self-defense:

> The first step made by natural and savage man toward civilization is the adoption of an artificial weapon, to compensate for the inferiority of those with which he is furnished by nature. Lacking the powerful jaws of the wolf, and the terrible claws of the tiger, the horns of the cattle, and the hoofs of the horse, he possesses in his hands and brains the faculty of invention, and the first use to which he puts it is the construction of a weapon. This comes before clothing and shelter, for food is the first necessity of the animal man, and without a weapon he cannot obtain animal food, but must live on roots and insects. The first mark of intelligence found in the most degraded savages is a weapon, and the first weapon he makes is a stick or club, a straight branch torn from a tree...[4]

Considering the club's popular association with "savagery" and primitivity, to understand why the desire existed to even learn—and teach—the use of an apparently anachronistic large, two-handed club, in an age

---

1 My own fencing master, Maestro Ramon Martinez, learned the use of a number of such traditional "antiquated" weapons from his German fencing master, *Maitre d'armes* Frederick Rohdes, who had learned them from his fencing master, *Maitre* Marcel Cabijos, and others in Europe. For a more detailed discussion, see Monstery, *Self- Defense for Gentleman and Ladies* (Berkeley: North Atlantic Books, 2015), vii-x. For a 19th century account of the survival of a living tradition of antiquated weapons, see Baron de Bazancourt, *Secrets de L'Epee* (Paris: Amyot, 1876), 189-91.

2 For example, see Alfred Hutton, *Old Swordplay* (Mineola, NY: Dover, 2002).

3 For instance, see the 5,500 year-old English "Thames Beater" in Meaghan Dyer and Linda Fibiger, "Understanding blunt force trauma and violence in Neolithic Europe: the first experiments using a skin-skull-brain model and the Thames Beater", *Antiquity,* December 6, 2017.

4 Monstery, *Self-Defense for Gentlemen and Ladies* , 141.

when so many other options were available and in vogue, requires some historical background and socio-cultural context. It is not our intention to provide a complete history of the the use of the club, or its many derivations, which is far beyond the scope of this small book.[5] Rather, we will briefly examine the popular image throughout time of a specific type of club—that is, of a long branch of largely natural form, steadily broadening in girth and weight towards its far end (or foible), which was an object of allure and romanticism from ancient times up through the nineteenth century.

CULTURAL SIGNIFICANCE OF THE CLUB IN EUROPE

Since the dawn of history, the club as a European weapon has firmly been associated with classical mythology—in particular, with the figure of Hercules, the ancient Roman equivalent of the Greek hero Heracles. As the story goes, since the early days of his infancy, Hercules engaged in a number of remarkable and superhuman feats of strength. So famous and memorable were these acts, that Hercules eventually came to embody the very concept of strength itself. Hercules's signature and iconic weapon was a large, knotted, two-handed club, which he used to battle and defeat various fearsome mythological creatures and nemeses. This club became closely associated with the hero to the degree that it forever became his *de facto* symbol, and golden "Hercules amulets"—shaped in the form of his club—became widely distributed throughout the Roman empire.[6]

Such amulets were especially prevalent in ancient Romanized Germany. According to chapter three of *Germania*, by the ancient Roman historian Tacitus:

> They have...the tradition of a Hercules of their country, whose praises they sing before those of all other heroes as they advance to battle. A peculiar kind of verse is also current among them, by the recital of which,

---

5 For a more thorough treatment of the evolution of the club throughout the world, and a survey of historical specimens, the reader is directed to the classic text: Richard F. Burton, *Book of the Sword* (London: Chatto & Windus, 1884), 1-52.

6 Joachim Werner, "Herkuleskeulen und Donar-Amulett", *Jahrbuch des Römisch-Germanischen Zentralmuseums Mainz* (1964): 11, 176-197; 31, 435-454.

Fig. 1. Bronze statuette of Hercules. Roman, 2nd to 3rd century A.D.. Getty Museum, Object number 71.AB.169.

Fig. 2. Statue of Hercules in the Chiaramonti Vatican Museum. 1ˢᵗ Century A.D. Roman copy of a Hellenistic original. Photo by James Anderson, 1859. Getty Museum, Object Number 84.XO.251.3.70.

Fig. 3. Cerberum domat Hercules, from Ovid's Metamorphoses, etched by Antonio Tempesta. Italian, 1606. Metropolitan Museum of Art, Accession Number: 51.501.3919.

Fig. 4. Hercules slaying the Hydra. Italian, 17th century. Metropolitan Museum of Art, Accession Number: 17.103.3

termed 'barding,' they stimulate their courage; while the sound itself serves as an augury of the event of the impending combat. For, according to the nature of the cry proceeding from the line, terror is inspired or felt: nor does it seem so much an articulate song, as the wild chorus of valor. A harsh, piercing note, and a broken roar, are the favorite tones; which they render more full and sonorous by applying their mouths to their shields... To Hercules and Mars they offer the animals usually allotted for sacrifice.[7]

Throughout the Middle Ages and Renaissance era, the figure of Hercules continued to capture the imagination of European writers, artists, craftsmen, storytellers, and nobles. During the Renaissance, the excavation and discovery of a number of ancient Roman statues such as the Farnese Hercules, the Hercules of the Forum Boarium, and the Hercules Mastai, became the inspiration for a new generation of artists, who continued to romanticize and popularize the figure of Hercules in a variety of mediums—typically depicting him draped with the skin of a lion, and posing with, or wielding, his massive two-handed club.

THE WILD MAN

At the same time, a very similar type of club was associated with another important figure deeply rooted in indigenous Northern European legend: that of the *woodwose*, or wild man[8]. Although its mythological origins are uncertain, and now lost in the mists of time, the woodwose resembled a human covered by long hair (or fur) across its entire body, excepting its hands, feet, and face. Later wild men were sometimes depicted without fur, but scantily clad in garlands of foliage. Female and juvenile woodwoses can also be found depicted in artwork of the period. The males were nearly always depicted with a large club of knobby, natural form—or sometimes, a sort of crude wooden mace—emphasizing the woodwose's primitive nature. Some artistic representations depict woodwoses holding a club in one hand, and a shield or small buckler in the other; still others, with spear, lance, or bow and arrow. Woodwoses figured prominently in manuscript marginalia, on playing cards, shield

---

7 Tacitus, *The Works of Tacitus: The Oxford Translation, Revised with Notes, Volume 2* (London: G. Bell, 1914), 289-90, 298.

8 In Old English, *wude-wāsa*; in German, *wilder mann*; in French, *homme sauvage*.

Fig. 5. Engraving of a Wild Man with club and shield, by Martin Schongauer. German, ca. 1470–1491. Metropolitan Museum of Art, Accession Number: 40.8.5.

engravings, in church relief sculpture, on furniture, and in artistic prints. They were particularly popular in heraldic coats-of-arms in Germany, further cementing the importance of the club in Germanic culture and permeating its popular imagery.[9] In addition, the club became generally associated with other legendary and mythological beings that were wild or primal in nature.

---

9   For a survey of the wild man in history and art, see Timothy Husband, *The Wild Man: Medieval Myth and Symbolism* (New York: Metropolitan Museum of Art, 1980).

Fig. 6. *"Wild Man in combat with a knight (the combat of Valentine and Namelos)" by Hans Burgkmair I. German, ca. 1500-1503. National Gallery of Art, Accession Number 1978.77.1.*

Fig. 7. Detail of ewer with Wild Man (wielding club) finial. German, probably made in Nuremberg, Franconia, ca. 1500. Metropolitan Museum of Art (Cloisters Collection), Accession Number 53.20.2.

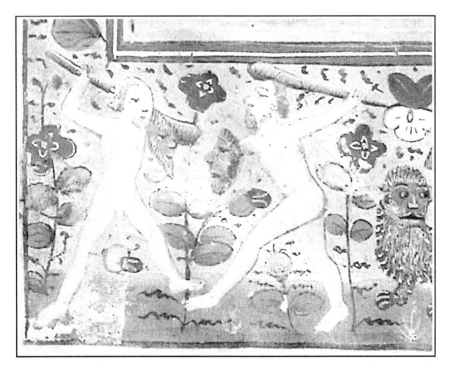

Fig. 8. Detail from manuscript leaf with peasants or wild men fighting with clubs and shields, from a Book of Hours. Last quarter of the 15th century, North French. Metropolitan Museum of Art, Accession Number 32.100.474b.

FIRST EUROPEAN TREATISES

During the medieval period, the club was also still used as a practical weapon in Germany and elsewhere in Europe, in a variety of contexts. Often associated with the peasantry, a large number of images can be found in the marginalia of illuminated manuscripts from the era, depicting naked or clothed peasants engaging in single combat with clubs, or with clubs and shields used in combination. A large, knobbed club of natural form, used as a weapon, can also be found in one of the earliest European fencing treatises, *Fior di Battaglia* (The Flower of Battle), by the Italian Fiore de'i Liberi, probably written and illustrated during the early 1400s. Towards the end of this treatise, a crowned fencing master is shown wielding two clubs simultaneously, one in each hand, and defending against the incoming attack of a spearman, which he does by hurling the club in his right hand at his adversary's head, beating the adversary's spear with the club in his left hand, and, finally, drawing a dagger with his remaining free hand and thrusting it into his attacker's chest (see Figs. 9 and 10).

Another context for club use during the period was that of the judicial duel, or trial-by-combat. A fifteenth century version of the Brabant Chronicle (written during the fourteenth century) contains a vivid illustration of such a duel, fought with single clubs, that probably took place during the thirteenth century. In his classic martial arts treatise of the mid-fifteenth century, fencing master Hans Talhoffer illustrates the use of the dueling shield in conjunction with a short but devastating single-handed club, or *kolben*, likely made of wood (see Figs. 11 and 12).[10] This same type of club is also shown in the irregular judicial duel pitting a man and woman against each other, in which the man is armed with the club, but is handicapped by being forced to stand in a pit waist-high, while the woman uses a cloth sling containing a stone that weighs four or five pounds. The same combination of short club and dueling shield, appearing quite similar to Talhoffer's, can also be found in the treatise of Paulus Kal, written during the final decades of the 1400s.[11]

Later, during the next century, a long, two-handed club of natural form appears in the German fencing treatise of Paulus Hector Mair. Referred to as a "peasant staff", this club appears quite distinct from a quarterstaff or long staff, and is similar to those seen in depictions of wild men, and of Hercules, as well as in Fiore's manuscript—that is, a long, heavy, shorn tree branch, with some knobs and irregularities left intact, and weighted towards the far end, or foible, of the weapon (see Figs. 13 and 14).[12]

Following the publication of Mair's treatise, virtually nothing more appears to have been published in Germany on the technical use of the club for at least several centuries. Then, during the mid-nineteenth century, a small explosion in the number of such treatises suddenly

---

10 According to Maestro Paul Macdonald of Edinburgh, the leading authority on the dueling shield and *kolben* in history and practice, the proportions of this weapon indicate a wooden construction (message to the author, Sept. 19, 2022).

11 See Paulus Kal, *Fechtbuch, gewidmet dem Pfalzgrafen Ludwig - BSB Cgm 1507,* Bayerische Staatsbibliothek.

12 See *Opus Amplissimum de Arte Athletica*, MSS Dresd.C.93/C.94, Sächsische Landes-bibliothek, Dresden, Germany.

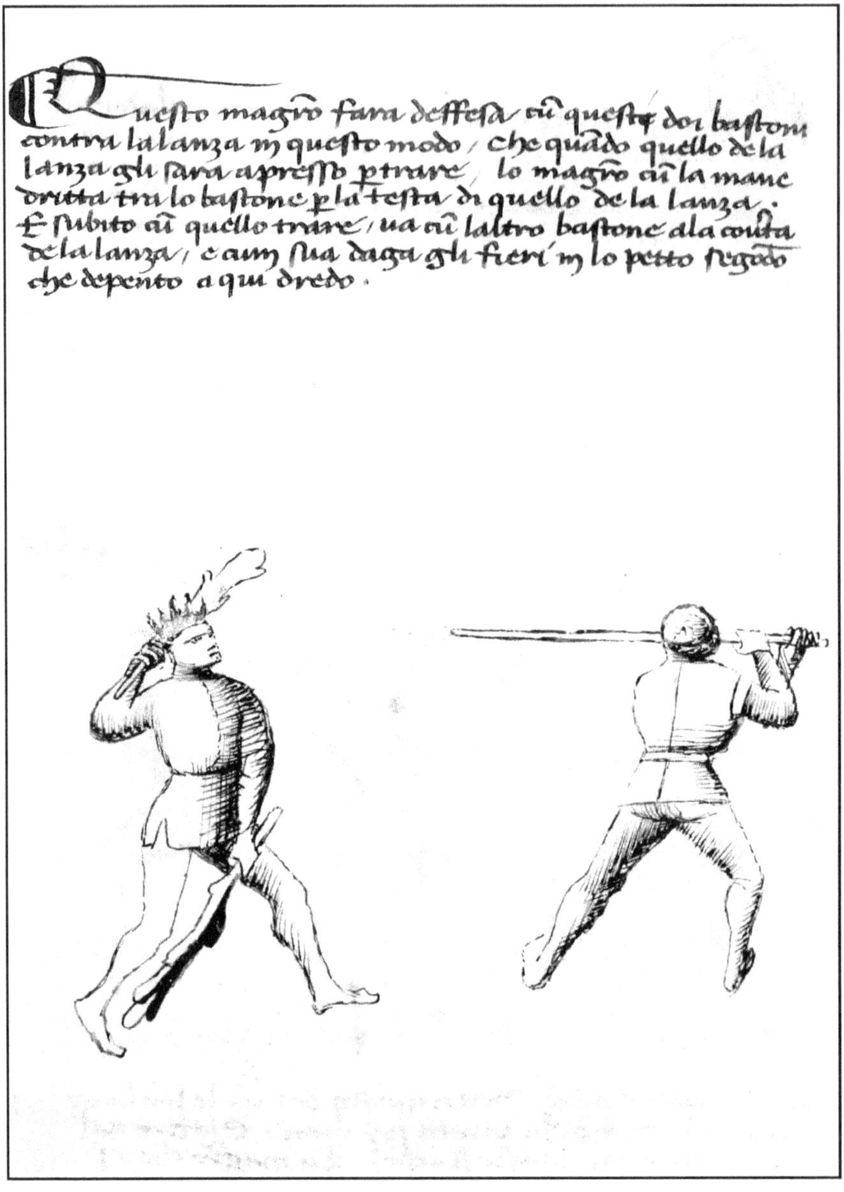

uesto magro fara deffesa cû questo doi bastoni
contra la lanza in questo modo, che quado quello de la
lanza gli sara apresso ptrare, lo magro cû la mane
dritta tra lo bastone p la testa di quello de la lanza.
E subito cû quello trare, ua cû laltro bastone ala costa
de la lanza, e aum sua daga gli fieri in lo petto segado
che depento a qui dredo.

Fig. 9. Detail of leaf from "The Flower of Battle" by Fiore Furlan dei Liberi da Premariacco. Italian, about 1340/1350 - before 1450. Getty Museum, Ms. Ludwig XV 13 (83.MR.183), fol. 31v.

Fig. 10. Another detail from Fiore (see previous Figure).

Fig. 11. Detail from the Fechtbuch of Hans Talhoffer, showing combatant armed with dueling shield and club. German, 16th century copy of a mid-15th century manuscript. Metropolitan Museum of Art, Accession Number 26.236.

Fig. 12. Another detail from the Fechtbuch of Hans Talhoffer, showing combatant with club (see previous Figure).

Fig. 13. Leaf from Opus Amplissimum de Arte Athletica *by Paulus Hector Mair. German, ca. 1542. Sächsische Landesbibliothek, Mscr.Dresd.C.93/94.*

Fig. 14. Another leaf from Mair (see previous Figure).

occurs, all between the years 1855 and 1862. Why was this so? Although it is difficult to theorize without speculating, a number of socio-cultural factors and possibilities are worth considering.

STRONGMEN AND STRONGWOMEN

The early nineteenth century had seen the birth of a new type of strong-man, a celebrity competitor who took part in contests, circuses, and exhibitions. Throughout the century, the phenomenon continued to grow, as a number of such strongmen began dressing and posing as Hercules, complete with the large two-handed club of natural form. Although it is not certain when this trend began, it is evident as early as 1834, when the image of Carl Rappo, a former aristocrat turned strongman from Innsbruck, Austria, was published in an engraving, now in the care of the British Museum. In this lithograph, Rappo is depicted executing a fencing lunge, while gripping a large club above his head with both hands, ready to strike. As proclaimed in the print's caption, he is dressed as the character of Hercules, wearing a vest, feather-headdress, skirt, belt and sandals.[13]

Similar motifs can be found in the portrait of Hippolyte Triat, a French strongman born in 1813. In a painting from the period, Triat is depicted bare-chested, much like a classical figure, and holds the end of a long, Herculean club of natural form (see Fig. 15). Although the painting is undated, Triat appears young, and as the height of his performing career was the 1830s and early 1840s, this seems like a probable date range for the portrait.

Although it is not clear if this tendency among strongmen to pose with, and wield, clubs, had any direct connection with the technical interest in the weapon that was to soon follow, at the very least, it does appear to point to a resurgence in popular representations of the club, and its symbolic connection with athleticism. Throughout the rest of the century, and well into the early twentieth, it was common for professional strongmen to dress and pose as figures from classical antiquity,

---

13 See *"Rappo, Herkules & Jongleur"* c. 1834 in the British Museum, Museum number 1892,0714.805.

Fig. 15. Portrait of Hippolyte Triat. French, date unknown.

Fig. 16. Italian strongman Felice Napoli. La Vie au Grand Air, *February 2, 1902.*

GRETE WOLFRAM
Preisgekrönte Athletin und Keulenschwingerin
Inhaberin des Deutschösterreichischen Damenrekord im Stoßen.

Fig. 17. Postcard from the author's collection. German, early 20th century.

often as part of so-called "studies" or tableaus. Although multiple figures from ancient history and legend—such as Samson, Apollo, Achilles, and Simon bar Kokhba—provided inspiration for these strongmen, the most popular was still always Hercules. Celebrity athletes such as the famous Prussian Eugene Sandow, George Jagendorfer, Louis Attila, Noel le Gaulois, Alfred Moss, and Felice Napoli, were all photographed while posing with massive clubs, often while wearing Hercules's signature lion or leopard skin.[14] Sometimes these clubs were plain, other times their surfaces were adorned with bands or studs, almost in the manner of a medieval weapon. As one club-swinging text of the period explained:

> The primal club, the cudgel, was easy to identify. In a way, it became a kind of yardstick of craftsmanship and taste, as people have tried at all times to make it more beautiful, sometimes through the addition of orna- ments, sometimes more effective through the addition of iron fittings, teeth, spikes, etc. Of course, if the weapon adorned the man, he adorned his weapon.[15]

Even women took part in this trend—as can be seen in a photograph of the German female athlete and club swinger, Grete Wolfram (see Fig. 17). Many treatises on strength cultivation also opened with a discussion of classical mythology, and regaled the reader with tales of ancient athletes (including Hercules), who were regarded as the ultimate models of athleticism worthy of emulation.[16] One popular brand of exercise club, which was of adjustable length, was even named after Hercules.[17]

Another factor in the sudden explosion of technical club treatises may have been the popularization of Indian and Persian club swinging in Europe which was taking place around the same time. Indian club, or *jori*, swinging had first arrived in Britain during the very early 1800s, brought by the British military who had witnessed the indigenous prac- tice while stationed in colonial India, and who had then modified those

---

14 See, for example, the various "club studies" done by Sandow, in Eugene Sandow, *Sandow on Physical Training: a Study in the Perfect Type of the Human Form* (New York: J.S. Tait, 1894), 28-29.

15 Heinrich Wortmann, *Das Keulenschwingen in Wort und Bild* (Hof: Verlag von Rud. Lion, 1885), 25.

16 See, for example, Guillaume Depping, *Merveilles de la force et de l'adresse: Agilité —souplesse—dextérité* (Paris: L. Hachette et Cie.1871), 3-12; Edmond Desbonnet, *Les rois de la force: histoire de tous les hommes forts depuis les temps anciens jusqu'à nos jours* (Paris: Libraire Berger-Levrault, 1911), vii-xi, 1-10.

17 The Hercules Graduated Gymnastic Club, Hercules Co., patented Mar. 1897, Boston.

Fig. 18. From Ravenstein's Volksturnbuch *(Frankfurt: a. M., J.D. Sauerländer's Verlag, 1868).*

techniques with ideas from European gymnastics. Club swinging did not come to Germany until a few decades later—in the late 1840s, to Leipzig.[18] However, even so, it was not until the 1860s that an original German treatise of any significance was published on the technique of club swinging that was rooted in the Eastern traditions. The first major work was by Turner director August Ravenstein, who had learned from both the British and French methods. Unlike the British method, which had drawn from Indian techniques, the French had been derived from methods of Persian *mil* swinging. Ravenstein reportedly blended the two, and then began modifying these techniques to create his own method.[19] Ravenstein describes how to swing, cut, and strike with the club (*keulenschlagen*) in the same manner as a staff. One highly distinctive technique that appears in his treatise is the act of swinging the large club above one's head with both hands, and then bringing it down in a "semi-circular cut" towards the ground (see Fig. 18). This type of movement would become a peculiarly German one, performed at large gymnastic festivals well into the 1930s, often with two clubs, one in each hand.

18 Wortmann, *Das Keulenschwingen in Wort und Bild* (Hof a. S.: Verlag von Rudolf Lion, 1905), 14-15.

19 *Deutsche Turnzeitung*, no. 44, 1864.

GERMAN CLUB TREATISES: 1855 - 1862

In 1855, the first German work distinctly treating of the club as both a weapon and a gymnastic exercise appeared—possibly the first work of any significant detail to be published in at least several centuries, since the Renaissance. This concise but sophisticated and nicely illustrated treatise on the use of the two-handed club was the work of Hugo Rothstein, a native German and ardent proponent of the Swedish method of gymnastics, which had been founded earlier in the century by the renowned gymnasiarch and fencing master, Pehr Henrik Ling.

Rothstein was born on August 28, 1810 in Erfurt, and became a soldier and artillery officer in the Prussian army. He was first exposed to Ling's method during a trip to Sweden in 1843. When he returned to Germany, he wrote an essay about Ling's gymnastics and the Swedish army that was published in the magazine *Der Staat*, which King Friedrich Wilhelm IV took note of. In 1845, accompanied by infantry Lieutenant Techow, Rothsetin was sent to Sweden by the Minister of War, Von Boyen, at the expense of the State, to acquire more intimate knowledge of Ling's gymnastics and to go through a course at Ling's Central Institute of Gymnastics (*Kungliga Gymnastiska Centralinstitutet*). For this purpose, Rothstein resided for a year in Stockholm, and, after that, three months in Copenhagen to observe the fencing and gymnastic instruction at the Danish Royal Institute of Military Gymnastics. Although Ling had died in 1839, during Rothstein's second sojourn in Stockholm, he saw much of Director Lars Branting and head teacher Augustus Georgii, and was also a frequent guest at the palace of King Oscar I. In the autumn of 1846, both officers were back in Berlin. Rothstein began work at once on a massive series of volumes about the Ling system, which appeared in installments between 1847 and 1859. The reports by Rothstein and Techow resulted in the founding in Berlin of a "Central Institute for Gymnastic Instruction in the Army" (*Zentralinstitut fur gymnastischen Unterricht inder Armee*), with the two aforementioned officers as teachers.[20] It was during this period, in 1855, that Rothstein

---

20 Fred Eugene Leonard, *A guide to the history of physical education* (Philadelphia and

published his short work on the use of the two-handed club, a method which he was actively teaching at his institute in Berlin.

Sadly, Rothstein's instruction was not to last. From the beginning of his return to Germany, Rothstein had taken to publicly condemning aspects of the popular gymnastic school in Germany at the time, the Turner physical culture movement, and their methods of exercise, a sentiment which runs throughout much of Rothstein's work. His conflict with the German Turners led to the so-called "parallel bar dispute", which began when Rothstein banned that apparatus from his school, causing outrage among the Turners. Petitions, memorials, and opinions for and against its use multiplied, and the discussion was widened to include the whole subject of the comparative merits of Ling-Rothstein gymnastics and the German Turner gymnastic school. Considerable opposition was aroused throughout Prussia and the question was taken to the House of Deputies, which at first was inclined to support Rothstein. The fact that the Prussian government initially supported the creation and maintenance of a Royal Berlin Institute based on a Swedish, and not Germanic, gymnastic method, can be explained by the fact that the German Turner movement was essentially a rebel nationalist movement, with Republican ideals that the Prussian monarchy was intensely suspicious of, and which had been banned by the German authorities at times.

The controversy, however, was ultimately decided to Rothstein's disadvantage by the highest medical authority in Prussia, the Royal Scientific Deputation for Medical Affairs. The apparatus was ordered restored, and in protest Rothstein withdrew from the school, and Berlin, in 1863.[21]

Before he did so, however, in 1862, Rothstein published yet one more short chapter on the use of the club. Mostly a simplified and condensed version of his first treatise, it nonetheless contained several new exercises with the club intended for physical development. Shortly thereafter, Rothstein returned to his hometown of Erfurt, where he died on March 23, 1865.

New York: Lea & Febiger, 1923), 122-124. Hugo Ziemssen, *Handbook of General Therapeutics, Volume 5* (N.Y.: William Wood, 1886), 40-41. K. Euler, *Encyklopädisches Handbuch des gesamten Turnwesens, B.VV.* (Vienna: Verlag von A. Pichler's Witwe & Sohn, 1894-6.). Rudolf Gasch, *Handbuch des gesamten Turnwesens und der verwandten Leibesübungen* (Wien & Leipzig: Pichler, 1920), 557.

21 Ibid.

Interestingly, during Rothstein's short reign in the German gymnastic world, a couple of other treatises on club exercise were published by other authors in Germany. In 1858, in Leipzig, Theodor Wittmaack, a doctor of medicine and surgery, published his *Popular Handbook of Diatetics*, containing "complete instructions for maintaining good health into old age, and ongoing rejuvenation of life".

Fig. 12, a.

Fig 19. Wittmaack's Figure 12.

Wittmaack treated of club exercise under the category of *Zimmergymnastik*, or "parlor gymnastics"— that is, exercise done indoors, within the confines of one's home. Wittmaack states that the movements are to be done first with empty hands, then whilst holding light dumbbells, and then, lastly, whilst holding the single club, which he describes as "the type used by athletes". He prescribes motions including arm-raises, arm extensions, and arm-circles, or circular swings with the arms. What follows is Wittmaack's brief technical instruction on the use of the club:

After a sufficient degree of skill in holding the club with the arm stretched out horizontally, in thrusting, throwing and circling with it, while standing firmly in place, has been acquired, the various positions are assumed which are customary in fencing (e.g B. Fig. 12, a): that is, the legs apart in an otherwise evenly weighted position: one leg forward, the other back; sideward lunge or leaning over to one side; also the club swings backwards, putting one leg back and making a side rotation of the body, the step backwards and forwards with legs apart, in both directions up and down, and right, left and straight ahead; the cut in the same directions, the high cut above the head, the cut to the ground, done as though it should almost strike the ground, but must not touch it.

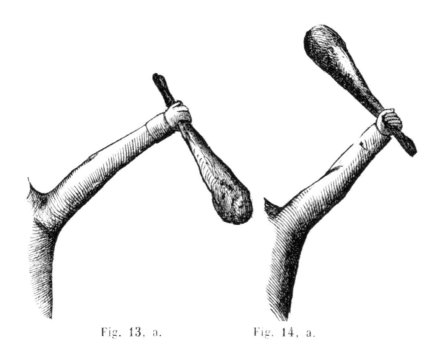

Fig. 13, a.   Fig. 14, a.

Fig. 20. From Wittmaack.

When a movement of this kind has been repeated four to eight times, the legs are quickly and tightly drawn together again, and the club brought like a sword to the side of the arm currently in use, so that the stump end of it touches the shoulder, and the hand gripping it is in the area just below the hip. (If the latter is still difficult at first, the club can be lowered to the ground so that the arm can rest.) It is best to rest the unused arm on the abdomen, below the pit of the heart, during the exercise. Incidentally, one must never fail to exercise both arms (Figs. 12, b, 13 and 14 a, b.) equally; the left arm, which is usually weaker, can, through exercise, acquire pretty much the same strength as the right.[22]

Unlike Rothstein, Wittmaack does not treat of the club as a weapon, though he does mention adopting a "fencing stance". Nor does his method resemble the Indian or Persian club swinging techniques that were just beginning to spread in Germany at the time. The club depicted is of natural form, like that of a roughly-hewn tree-branch, and the stance

22 Theodor Wittmaack, *Populäres Handbuch der Diätetik: oder vollständige Anweisung zur Erhaltung der Gesundheit und fortlaufenden Verjüngung des Lebens bis in das späte Alter* (Leipzig: E. Schäfer, 1858).

Fig. 12, b.

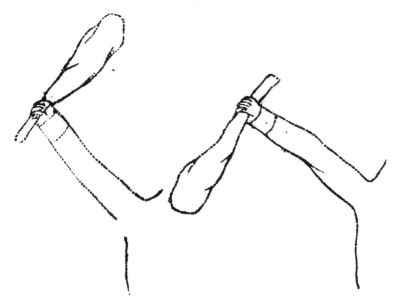

Fig. 14, b.   Fig. 13, b.

Fig. 21. From Wittmaack.

is similar to that used in European cavalry exercises done while standing dismounted. It is uncertain if Wittmaack was influenced at all by Rothstein—nor is the instruction in his text particularly clear or precise. However, it is worth noting that approximately five years later, a position strikingly similar to Wittmack's "Figure 12" was illustrated in Ravenstein's *Volksturnbuch*, with a stave or stick in place of a club.[23]

"TURNER AND MILITARY GYMNASTICS"

In 1861, while Rothstein was still in charge of the Central Institute in Berlin, yet another text appeared treating of the club exercises, published in Neustadt by one Ferdinand Wilhelmi, an instructor of both gymnastics and fencing, who had recently come to Germany from Switzerland. Wilhelmi's book on *Turner and Military Gymnastics* was intended for broad use: in schools, *Turnvereins* (local Turner clubs), and in the army. A brief section of the book, only one page long, contains a series of club exercises. These exercises utilized both one-handed and two-handed grips with a single club, as well as techniques performed with two clubs, used in each hand simultaneously, similar to Indian club swinging. Most notably, it also integrated a mixture of fencing *moulinets*, lunges, deep knee-bends, footwork, and many characteristics of Swedish gymnastics which had recently begun influencing Turner methods—in fact, Wilhelmi's text appears to be one of the first to include such techniques with the club. His method also contains thrusting techniques, walking, and running exercises done with clubs in hand, the latter of which also appears in Rothstein's later 1862 exercise. Like Wittmaack's previous work, Wilhelmi's is somewhat mysterious, and it is unclear if his exercise—with a diverse combination of elements found in other methods, both Western and Eastern in origin—was modified by himself from something pre-existing, or if it was a blend of several methods. Unfortunately, his text contains no illustrations of his exercises.[24]

---

23 August Ravenstein, *Volksturnbuch: im Sinne von Jahn, Eiselen und Spiess, und nach den in Berlin am 11. August 1861 von der Versammlung deutscher Turnlehrer angenommenen Grundsätzen.* (Frankfurt: a. M., J.D. Sauerländer, 1868). 440.

24 Ferdinand Wilhelmi, *Turnen und Militär-Gymnastik zu Uebungstafeln bearbeitet für Schulen, Vereine und die Armee: Gewidmet der deutschen Turnerei und Wehrhaftmachung. Mit lithographischer Abbildung einer Turnschanze* (Neustadt a. d. s.: D. Kranzbühler jun., 1861), 4.

"CLUB SWINGING" IN GERMANY

Although only tangentially relevant to the focus of this book, it would be remiss not to mention the impact of fencing techniques on "club swinging" in Germany—by "club swinging", meaning the form of club exercise rooted in Indian and Persian traditions. Although these Eastern traditions had originally arisen from, or had been inspired by, the martial use of the club in Persia and India in ancient times, since then they had evolved into their own entities, primarily used as tools for physical development, not for self-defense. The theory, fundamentals, and motions of Indian and Persian club swinging are, therefore, quite different from Rothstein's fencing-based method. Moreover, the clubs used by German club swingers during the mid nineteenth century tended to be far heavier (seven to twenty-one pounds)[25], in contrast to Rothstein's clubs (two and three-quarters to three pounds), as the objectives of the former methods were much more focused on strength building during those decades.

As stated earlier, as far as we know, such Eastern-rooted traditions first appeared in Germany during the 1840s. This form of club swinging struggled to obtain a foothold in the region until the efforts of Ravenstein, who published his first *Volksturnbuch* in 1863. From that time onwards, club swinging grew steadily in popularity throughout the region, eventually resulting in its mass-adoption by the Turner physical culture movement, and in the publication of a number of other original texts on the subject, which were increasingly German, and less Eastern, in nature. By the turn of the century, German club swinging authors felt that their systems had evolved to such a degree that they bore little resemblance to the original methods from which they had arisen:

> The history of the club has very little to do with our club swinging today, and we only hear very occasionally that the club of foreign peoples or in earlier times would have found a similar use as today.[26]

---

25 Wortmann (1905), 19.
26 Ibid., 13.

These later German authors were also quite aware of the prior existence of Rothstein's more martial treatment of the club. However, they mostly rejected any connection with it as well, insisting:

> It is unnecessary to go into these exercises [of Rothstein] any further, because real fencing with clubs differs completely from our club swinging and hardly seems feasible with wooden clubs.[27]

Indeed, there seems to be no fundamental connection between Rothstein's method, and the Indo-Persian-Germanic methods of the mid to late nineteenth century—although, interestingly, one such author does note: "Rothstein's method, using one meter-long clubs, is very similar to the stick-striking (*stockschlagen*)[28] techniques described by Ravenstein."[29] This same author, Heinrich Wortmann, also peppers his text throughout with ornamental chapter headings containing images of European medieval maces and morningstars, and briefly discusses the use of those weapons in German medieval history.[30]

While these authors may have protested any connection with Rothstein's method, or to

Fig. 22. From Wortmann's Das Keulen-schwingen (1885).

---

27 Ibid., 17.

28 For Ravenstein's *stockschlagen,* see August Ravenstein, *Volksturnbuch: im Sinne von Jahn, Eiselen und Spiess, und nach den in Berlin am 11. August 1861 von der Versammlung deutscher Turnlehrer angenommenen Grundsätzen* (Frankfurt: a. M., J.D. Sauerländer's Verlag, 1863), 404-413.

29 Wortmann (1905), 17.

30 Wortmann (1885), 20-24.

fencing, the fact of the matter is that by 1885, various technical influences from fencing had made their way into Germanic club-swinging, most likely in part through the influence of the Swedish method.[31] For instance, in a club-swinging text published that year, one can find techniques described as head parries, executed while gripping a club with both hands (see Fig. 22).[32] Club exercises with fencing lunges (or more accurately, the Swedish "fallout" position, which had been derived from fencing) are also shown, similar to what was described by Wilhelmi in his treatise published twenty-four years prior.

It is also worth noting that such club swinging exercises were recommended as preparatory and adjunct conditioning for fencing itself, by authors of German fencing literature. In 1894, a treatise on saber fencing by Gustav Ritter von Arlow and Lieutenant Franz Litomyský recommended club exercises as "a very good means of preparation" for saber fencing, and which "require less space."[33] And in 1898, another German author claimed that regular exercise with the clubs would enable "one to use saber, bayonet and lance with greater security and power."[34]

THE KAISER AND THE CLUB

It is also entirely possible that these fencing positions were brought into later club-swinging exercises directly via Rothstein's method—which, the evidence suggests, did not actually become extinct upon his death.

Only three years after Rothstein's departure from the Berlin Institute, and one year after his death, in January 1866, the then-military teacher at the Central Gymnastics Institute, First Lieutenant Von Dresky, later colonel and director of the Royal Military Gymnastics Institute, became a gymnastics teacher for the seven-year-old Prince Wilhelm, future German Emperor. According to one account:

---

31 Swedish footwork and calisthenics had originally been introduced into the German Turner school during the 1840s under the term "free exercises" by Adolf Spiess, who modified Jahn's method significantly, creating a fracture in the school between adherents of Jahn and adherents of Spiess. Adolf Spieß, *Die Lehre der Turnkunst: Das Turnen in den Freiübungen für beide Geschlechter* (Basel: Richter, 1840).

32 Wortmann (1885), 112.

33 Gustav Ritter von Arlow and Litomyský, *Systematisches Lehrbuch für den Unterricht im Säbelfechten* (Wien und Leipzig: Wilhelm Braumüller, 1894), 46.

34 "Anleitung für Keulenübungen" in *Militär-Wochenblatt,* June, 1898, 185.

Fig. 23. Kaiser Wilhelm II, physical culture enthusiast, pictured on the cover of Der Turner *magazine, one year prior to attending a public exhibition of Rothstein's club-fencing method. From the author's collection.*

The physical training of Kaiser Wilhelm II is well known...his Gymnastics instruction took place in Berlin in the winter in the former auditorium of the French Gymnasium, and in summer in the park of the new palace near Potsdam. Since 1868, Prince Heinrich also took part in gymnastics, and just as he had a special preference for exercises on the erected mast in the gymnasium, so did Prince Wilhelm for all military exercises. Already in the second year he was able to finish swimming, he became a very skilled rifleman, a good marksman, a capable fencer—especially using cutting weapons—a skillful rower, and also a dashing horseman. The gymnastics lessons lasted until 1875, in which year the two princes went to Kassel. However, Kaiser Wilhelm repeatedly proved that he remained inclined towards gymnastics.

Evidently some of Rothstein's method of using the club survived at the Royal Berlin Institute, likely through his former students or instructors. Decades later, in 1890, it was reported that the now Kaiser Wilhelm II attended the gymnastics performances of both the Military Gymnastics Institute and the Royal Gymnastics Teacher Training Institute, and was also present at the gymnastics in the former institute on February 25th.[35] On March 28th he attended the final performance at the gymnasium, recounted as follows:

With the usual punctuality, the Kaiser pulled up in front of the institution at 12:30 noon; Adjutant Major von Hulsen had already appeared ahead of him; he was accompanied by the adjutant, Naval Captain Freiherr von Senden. Upon entering the hall, he was greeted by the Minister, Director Dr. Köpke, the undersigned teacher, to whom he shook hands, he first had the teachers of the institution introduced to him, greeted senior teacher Eckler and then walked down the rows of the students, learning from each one their name, place of residence and position. This time calisthenics and fencing were abandoned; Teacher Gauhl began with iron wand exercises: simple forms, the value of which lay in absolutely correct execution. Turner instructor Otto led the club exercises again; there were two sets of exercises: club swinging (*keulenschwingen*) in a variety of ways, after [Heinrich] Wortmann, and club-fencing (*keulenfechten*) after Rothstein. The exercises went excellently and the club-fencing was particularly

---

35 *Zeitschrift für Gesundheitsfürsoge und Schulgesundheitspflege, Vol. 3* (Hamburg & Leipzig: L. Voss., 1890), 350.

pleasing, with or without lunging, and also in connection with thrusting, was applauded by the Kaiser and those present.[36]

The magazine *Der Turner* described these club demonstrations in slightly greater detail:

> The Kaiser picked up a club himself and found the exercises with it to be just as tonic for the chest as it was for the arm, and especially the wrist. What attracted the Kaiser's attention the most was the fencing led by the assistant teacher, Witt. Fencing assaults were executed with great aplomb by a number of pairs.[37]

Another source reporting on the event noted that the Kaiser

> was particularly interested in club-fencing and club-swinging. He took up a club himself, made some movements with it, and said that these exercises were as strengthening for the chest as they were for the arm and especially the wrist. May the Kaiser's example inspire the German school youth to renewed enthusiasm for their physical education![38]

As late as 1893, it was noted that both Rothstein's method of club-fencing was considered a separate discipline from club-swinging exercises—and that the former pre-dated the latter, with club-swinging not being introduced until 1889:

> In the early 1850s at the central gymnasium in Berlin, club-fencing was taught by the teaching director Major Rothstein. In 1889, club swinging was introduced in the gymnastic teacher training institute that had grown out of the central gymnasium. Presented to the Emperor in the spring of 1890 in the closing performance of His Majesty, it aroused his lively interest. But he was not unfamiliar with the exercises...The exercises are now widely practiced in schools.[39]

---

36 Euler & Eckler, *Monatsschrift für das Turnwesen, mit besonderer Berücksichtigung des Schulturnens und der Gesundheitspflege, Volumes 9-10* (Berlin: R. Gaertners Verlagsbuchhandlung, 1890), 179.

37 *Der Turner, No. 8,* 1890.

38 *Zeitschrift für Gesundheitsfürsoge und Schulgesundheitspflege,* 350.

39 *Jahresberichte über das höhere Schulwesen, Vol. 8, Jahr 1893* (Berlin: R. Gaertner, 1894), XVI, 36.

Fig. 24. German postcard, early 20ᵗʰ century, from the author's collection.

THE TWENTIETH CENTURY

As the decades passed, within the German school of gymnastics, additional fencing positions and movements were adapted for use in group club exercises, which took on a more combative appearance. Especially popular were synchronized mass drills, timed to music, in which one group of practitioners would lunge and attack with the club (or clubs), while the other group would parry or defend—sometimes while kneeling or crouching, to make the exercise more strenuous. This was done with the practitioners wielding single clubs (using both one-handed and two-handed grips), as well as with double clubs, one in each hand. Regarding the latter, one such surviving exercise is an Exhibition Drill, performed by nine Turners from St. Louis, Missouri, at the 11ᵗʰ national German Turner Festival, held at Frankfurt, Germany, in 1908:

Third Group:
  1. Exercise.
  a) Lunge forward left and raise left club forward oblique upward, the right club oblique downwards backwards... 1 — 4
  b) 1. Files: Lunge forward right, and raise right club to strike, & lower left club oblique backwards.

Fig. 25. Postcard from the author's collection. Switzerland, 1909.

     2. Files: Stride backwards left and kneel right, and raise right club to "cover" head, left oblique downwards backwards.... 5 — 8

     c) Like a and b.... 9 — 12

     d) Fundamental position.... 13 — 16

     Repeat a — d, but in b 1. and 2. files change exercises.... 17 — 32[40]

One year later, in 1909, an exercise similar to the above one, but utilizing large, two-handed clubs, was illustrated on the postcard for a massive gymnastic festival in Lausanne, Switzerland (see Fig. 25). An article published in advance of the event indicated that the practitioners of this club exercise were from Le Grütli and Wädenswil.[41] The very unusual and distinctive long, spiked clubs used by participants were probably meant to commemorate, or allude to, a regional historical event known as *Die Keulen in Verzweiflung* ("The Clubs of Despair"), which took place in the Prettigua Valley in Switzerland on May 27, 1622. In response to a brutal Austrian invasion that had seen the burning of villages and the massacring of men, women, and children, the local inhabitants rose up *en masse*, and, armed with enormous clubs, swooped

---

40 Henry Bauer Camann, *Indian club exercises and exhibition drills, arranged for the use of teachers and pupils in high school classes, academies, private schools, colleges, gymnasiums, normal schools, etc.* ([Chicago, Ill.: 1910]), 69.

41 *Journal Suisse*, May 27, 1909.

Fig. 26. "Die Keulen in Verzweiflung." Engraving, circa 1840.

down on their tyrants, knocking down a very large number of them. Illustrations from nineteenth century texts describing this event, and published in Lausanne, depict the inhabitants wielding clubs strikingly similar to those used at the 1909 festival in the same city (see Fig. 26).[42]

Another such exercise, somewhat more elaborate, was published in 1926 by Professor Robert Nohr, a German American Turner from Wisconsin. Fortunately, his directions are some of the more detailed ones still extant for this genre of exercise:

Exercise I.
    Count I. Number one, face left, step left forward and raise arms forward, grasping club with both hands. Number two, face right, lunge right forward, grasp club with both hands and bend arms to strike over head.

42 Favey, *Histoire suisse racontée à mes jeunes amis pour servir de continuation aux histoires racontées par Lamé Fleury: par un véritable ami de la jeunesse: utile si je puis* (Lausanne: Au dépot bibliographique de J. Chantrens, 1849), 149.

Count 2. Number one, lunge right forward, and bend arms to strike over head. Number two, kneel left and straighten arms forward.

Count 3. Number one, strike forward touching club of partner. Number two, bend trunk left, place left hand on floor and bend right arm to semi-circle over head to parry blow of partner.

Count 4. Both return to positions as in count 2.

Count 5. Number one, same as count 3. Number two, bend trunk right, place right hand on floor and bend left arm to semi-circle over head to parry blow of partner.

Count 6. Both return to position as on count 2.

Count 7. Number one, straighten right knee, step right backward and lower arms forward. Number two, return to position as on count one.

Count 8. Number one, replace left foot, face right, grasp club in left hand and return to starting position. Number two, same as number one but face left replacing club in right hand.[43]

Other club exercises integrating combative movements consisted of solo drills in which the practitioner made continuous motions attacking and defending with the club, sometimes with a *staccato* tempo, other times flowing into one another, combined with a mixture of fencing lunges, passes, and physical culture footwork.[44] Sometimes these positions would be held for extended periods of time, as part of a tableau or "plastic pose" before an audience. One particularly striking image, from the book *Der Turnwart*, published during the early twentieth century, shows a student with a club executing a *passata soto* (a technique from the Italian

Bild 23.

Fig. 27. From Gasch's 33 Turntafeln.

---

43 *Mind & Body*, Sept.-Oct. 1925.
44 For instance, see Rudolf Gasch, *33 Turntafeln für das Keulenschwingen* (Leipzig: Max Hesse, 1899). Sample image shown in Fig. 27.

Fig. 28. Defensive position with club, from Der Turnwart *(author's collection).*

Fig. 29. Fighting pictorial position from Der Turnwart.

Fig. 30. Fighting pictorial position from Der Turnwart. *Both postures can be found in the German Turner calisthenics (freiübungen) of the same era.*

Fig 31. A passata soto with club, from Der Turnwart.

school of fencing) against another student who is in a German calisthenic lunge (with rear fist closed) while extending a club in his lead hand (see Fig. 31).[45]

It is important to note that these exercises, though martial in appearance, were not intended to train the practitioners in actual self-defense methods or techniques, as Rothstein's had done. In his Turner *handbuch*, club swinger Rudolf Gasch explained that

> Real club-fencing [since Rothstein] has never been heard from again. Cutting motions and parries as preliminary exercises for fencing are often performed, but a real defense against blows is not possible with our clubs.[46]

Rather, these martial fencing techniques were being altered and adapted for the purposes of mental and physical development within the club swinging syllabi and approaches of their respective methods. As one prominent author of the period explained:

45 Georg Benedix, *Der Turnwart. Hilfsbuch für den praktischen Übungsbetrieb* (Leipzig: Arbeiter-Turnverlag A.G.; 1921), 73-75.
46 Rudolf Gasch, *Handbuch des gesamten Turnwesens und der verwandten Leibesübungen* (Vienna & Leipzig: Pichler, 1920), 327.

Fig. 32. "Hunt of the Wild Man". Historical Sportfest performed by the German Turnverein of Schluckenau (now Šluknov), August 27, 1899. Postcard from the author's collection.

What is the point of one of the most primitive close-range weapons of our ancestors, the club, in a time when the Mauser rifle carries its deadly projectile into the heart of the enemy at twelve-hundred paces and more? Not amidst the turmoil of wild battles should it again dash fatally, not to kill wild game in the merry hunt; no, in a changed form, coming closer to the original weapon, the club makes its return to Germany—it wants to be in the familiar home of the parlor gymnasts and in the places where our German youth, true to the old motto: *'Mens sana in corpore sano!'*[47] strive to strengthen the body through swinging and jumping—contributing in a modest way to the fact that, in addition to skill, physical strength finds cultivation and a home.[48]

---

47 This is the motto (taken from the original ancient Latin, by the poet Juvenal) of the German Turner movement; in English it reads: "A Sound Mind in a Sound Body!"
48 Wortmann (1905), 6.

Fig. 33. Pehr Henrik Ling (1776-1839).

II.

NOTES ON THE TREATISE

O f all the treatises we have heretofore mentioned, Rothstein's 1855 text, presented in full in the remainder of this book, is of the most interest from a martial perspective, as it is possibly the most detailed and erudite technical treatment of the use of the club as a weapon to have been published in Europe. Unlike the other club treatises of the period, nearly all of Rothstein's positions and motions are very clearly founded upon concepts of offense and defense, and to all appearances, his work seems to present something very much like a combat method. However, Rothstein himself makes clear that the primary objective of his method is self-development, not self-defense—due in no small part to the fact that he deems fencing with his clubs, or using them in earnest against a fully resisting opponent, to be simply too dangerous for the practitioners, even if done whilst wearing robust protective equipment. He nevertheless provides detailed instructions for how to construct specialized training clubs out of leather and horsehair for use in fencing, including in the free assault (*contrafechten*), and admits that training in his method will be both practical and useful, because "in the event of an emergency, a club (or a club-like weapon), such as may be at hand, would then be able to be used [by the practitioner] with skill and safety." He refers to this method, alternately, as both "club handling" (*keulenführung*) and "club fencing" (*keulenfechten*).[49] The purpose of his method is thus dualistic—primarily for self-development, but also for self-defense.

To fully appreciate this apparent dualism, it is important to understand the origins of Rothstein's ideas, and the framework of the system in which his method was taught: that of Ling's Swedish method.

As previously recounted, Rothstein was an avid disciple of the Swedish method of gymnastics founded by Pehr Henrik Ling in Stockholm during the beginning of the nineteenth century. It is worth noting that, during this time, the term "gymnastics" simply referred to any type of physical training—or, as Noah Webster's Dictionary of 1831 defined it, "the art of performing athletic exercises"—i.e., encompassing activities done in a gymnasium. Ling took this concept much further by creating a truly holistic system for the cultivation of mind, body, and spirit, which he termed "rational gymnastics"—that is, exercise which was not random or aimless, but which was systematic, scientific, and contained an expressed, coherent purpose (primarily, the cultivation of health). His vast method was divided and organized into the following branches:

1. *Educational Gymnastics* — by means of which man learns to bring his body under the control of his own will (i.e., for control of self).

2 . *Military Gymnastics* — in which man seeks, by means of an external object, i.e., a weapon, or also by means of his own bodily powers, to subjugate another external will (i.e., fencing, wrestling, boxing, etc.).

3. *Medical Gymnastics* — whereby the individual, either on his own, in a suitable position, or by means of the assistance of others and effective movements, seeks to overcome the sufferings that have arisen in his body due to abnormal conditions (i.e., physical therapy and massage).

4 . *Aesthetic Gymnastics* — through which the individual seeks to physically express his inner being, thoughts, and feelings (i.e., movements for artistic expression).[50]

---

49 Rothstein refers to *keulenfechten* in his teacher's training manual, *Leitfaden zur Instruction gymnastischer Gehülsen* (Berlin: Schroeder: Kaiser, 1860), 54.
50 Per Henrik Ling, *Gymnastikens allmänna grunder* (Upsala: Leffler och Sebell, 1834).

Fig. 34. Foil versus staff weapons in the system of Pehr Henrik Ling. From Tollin's Neue Illustrirte Fechtschule, *Grimma & Leipzig, 1851.*

It is the second category, Military Gymnastics (*wehrgymnastik*), to which Rothstein's method of club use originally belonged, as he unambiguously states in the opening sentence of his treatise: "In its proper sense, the use of the club belongs to Military Gymnastics."[51] Organizing his method according to the same divisions as Ling, Rothstein further subdivides Military Gymnastics—the martial arts—into the following categories and weapons:

> Cut-fencing (*hiebfechten*):
>> with a one-handed weapon: saber, etc.
>> with a two-handed weapon: club, etc.
>
> and
>
> Thrust-fencing (*stossfechten*):
>> with a one-handed weapon: smallsword, dagger, etc.
>> with a two-handed weapon: bayonet-rifle, pike, etc.[52]

Thus, when Rothstein entitles his club treatise, "The Method of Handling the Club as a Gymnastic Exercise", his use of the word "gymnastic" (*gymnastik*) may be understood to encompass the martial arts as well as, potentially, other branches of gymnastics (as it turns out,

---

51 Hugo Rothstein, *Athenaeum für rationelle Gymnastik, Volume II* (Berlin: E.H. Schroeder, 1855), 143.
52 Hugo Rothstein, *Die Geräth-Uebungen und Spiele aus der pädagogischen Gymnastik* (Berlin: E.H. Schroeder, 1862), 2.

Fig. 35. Rothstein's saber technique, or hiebfechten (cut-fencing), from Das Stoss- und Hiebfechten mit Degen und Säbel, *Berlin, 1863.*

Rothstein utilized the club in a total of three of the four branches). Perfectly in line with the philosophy of Ling, the objective of Rothstein's martial arts was not only preparation for self-defense, but comprised the cultivation of mind, body, and spirit—as he himself explained in his larger treatise on Military Gymnastics: "in terms of its purpose and thus its ethical significance, Military Gymnastics proves to be a justified and necessary or obligatory activity not merely for the assertion of a bodily or earthly self-preservation, but for the sake of a spiritual one."[53]

In a subsequent text, Rothstein indicated that all the above-mentioned weapons (foil, smallsword, saber, dagger, bayonet-rifle, spear, and club)

53 Hugo Rothstein, *Die Gymnastik nach dem Systeme des schwedischen Gymnasiarchen P.H. Ling: Die Wehrgymnastik, Volume 4* (Berlin: Schroeder, 1851), 3.

Lektionsplan für das dritte Quartal des fünften Unterrichtscursus.

Eleven	Stunden	Montag	Dienstag	Mittwoch	Donnerstag	Freitag	Sonnabend
Militair.	7 – 8	Physiologie und Diätetik			Physiologie und Diätetik		
	8 – 9	Bajonetfechten	Vorträge über Gymnastik	Rüstübungen	Vorträge über Gymnastik	Instruktions-stunde	Degenfechten
	9¼ – 10¼	Lanzenführung, resp.Stabspringen	Degenfechten	Säbelfechten	Degenfechten	Säbelfechten	Rüstübungen
	½11 – ½12	Zur Disposition	Rüstübungen	Zur Disposition	Bajonetfechten	Lanzenführung, resp.Stabspringen	Zur Disposition
Civil.	7 – 8	Physiologie und Diätetik	Freiübungen		Physiologie und Diätetik		
	8 – 9	Rüstübungen	Vorträge über Gymnastik	Instruktions-stunde	Vorträge über Gymnastik	Degenfechten	Rüstübungen
	9¼ – 10¼	Bajonetfechten, resp.Stabspringen	Rüstübungen	Rüstübungen	Rüstübungen	Instruktions-stunde	Degenfechten
	½12 – ½1	Zur Disposition	Bajonetfechten, resp.Stabspringen	Zur Disposition	Freiübungen,resp. Keulenführung	Rüstübungen	Zur Disposition

Fig. 36. Rothstein's "Plan of Lessons for the third Quarter of the fifth Teaching course", listing a club-handling class on Thursdays.

were being taught at his Central Institute (*Königliches Centralinstitut*) in Berlin, in which he had a fencing salle (*fechtsaal*) sixty feet long, thirty feet wide, with an asphalt floor.[54] He elaborated:

> Only in the fencing hall are the fencing exercises almost exclusively prac-ticed. The weapons and other equipment required for this, which are avail-able in abundance, are usually located in lockable cupboards and are only handed out for each use during the lessons.

Rothstein states that the use of all of "these fencing exercises...are included in the lessons at the Royal [Berlin] Central Institute" for both civil and military trainees, including "the handling of the club."[55] For the semester spanning 1855 and 1856, Rothstein provided a chart of his weekly "Plan of lessons for the third quarter of the fifth teaching course", in which he indicated how his club-fencing class fit into the schedule (alongside other classes on the use of the bayonet, smallsword, lance, saber, and calisthenics), on Thursdays around noon (see Fig. 36).[56]

---

54 Asphalt rose in popularity during the 1830s, and was thought excellent material "for forming level and durable terraces" in palaces, rather than streets. *The Mechanics' Magazine*, Vol. 29. London: W.A. Robertson. April 7–September 29, 1838. p. 176.

55 Hugo Rothstein, *Die Königliche Central-Turn-Anstalt zu Berlin* (Berlin: Mittler, 1862), 6, 27.

56 Hugo Rothstein, *Athenaeum für rationelle Gymnastik, Volume IV* (Berlin: Verlag von E. H. Schroeder, 1857), 93.

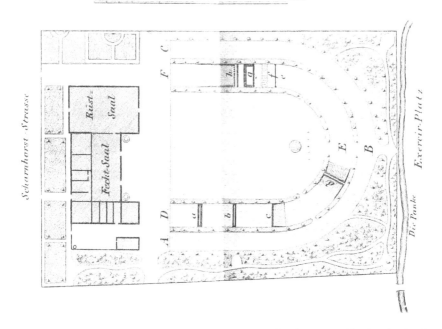

Grundriss des ganzen Grundstücks

Fig. 37. Map of the Königliches Centralinstitut. The fencing salle (Fecht-Saal) where Rothstein taught the use of the club can be seen at center left.

In 1857, Rothstein reviewed an earlier gymnastic treatise authored by Francisco Amorós y Ondeano, a Franco-Spanish ex-soldier who ran a prominent gymnasium in Paris.[57] In his review of this text, Rothstein distinguished between his own combative club exercise, and that of the Persian *mil* advocated by Amorós:

> These exercises are borrowed from the modern-day Persians, and have already been adopted by Clias and Amoros. They are made a fuss of in France; for our part, however, we cannot find them so praiseworthy and recommendable. The name of the exercise refers to the device used, whose name *Mil* we most appropriately translate as "Schwängel"[58] and not, as has usually been done, "club" (*keule*). When you hear the term "club" you must think of a powerful, slashing weapon that is wielded with two hands; and thus, under the term club exercises (*keulen-übungen*), you

---

57 Francisco Amoros, *Nouveau manuel complet d'éducation physique, gymnastique et morale. Atlas / par le Colonel Amoros* (Paris: Roret, 1848).
58 *Schwängel:* A handle, pendulum or clapper.

can expect such exercises through which the use of the club for club combat (*keulengefecht*) is learned. The *Exercices des Mils* or the Schwängel exercises, on the other hand, do not refer at all to such a fight, or to the use of the apparatus as a weapon.* The apparatus for the [*Mil*] exercises under discussion here is not really designed like a club, and is not wielded with two hands as aforesaid, but rather with one in each hand, i.e. two of them are handled at the same time.

* [My] practice lessons for the handling of the club, which are given in the second volume of the second volume of the *Athenaeum*, are compiled with this latter determination in mind.[59]

Fig. 38. Hugo Rothstein (1810-1865).

In 1862, Rothstein issued another illustrated club exercise, in which he explained how the management of the club can also be an important part of not only Military Gymnastics, but of Educational Gymnastics as well. In the original Swedish method, the branch known as Educational Gymnastics (*pädagogische gymnastik*) consisted overwhelmingly of calisthenics (*freiübungen*), with some exercises on stationary apparatus (*rüstübungen*) such as stall bars and ropes, while eschewing the use of popular handheld exercise tools such as wands, Indian clubs, barbells, and dumbbells. Rothstein seems to have departed from this orthodox philosophy, however, in heartily recommending and propounding the use

---

59 Rothstein, *Athenaeum für rationelle Gymnastik, Volume IV*, 263.

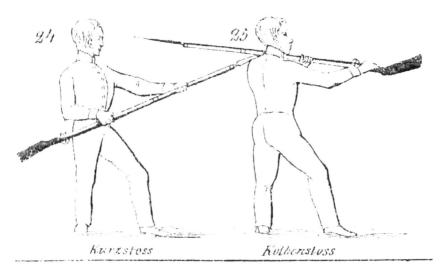

Fig. 39. Bayonet fencing according to Rothstein's Die Wehrgymnastik, *1851.*

of such portable apparatus (*geräthübungen*) within the branch of Educational Gymnastics. He explains with regard to the club:

§. 1. In the system of rational gymnastics, exercises with portable apparatus are understood to mean those exercises in which the practitioner, as in calisthenics, moves on the usual ground and finds his support points on that, and in the feet, but at the same time carries small, portable hand-held devices (staves, hoops, balls, weapons, etc.), the handling of which essentially determines the exercise movements in quantitative and qualitative respects...

§. 2. The portable apparatus exercises can be divided into two main groups: those that belong to Military Gymnastics and consist in using the weapons for fencing practice, generally called "fencing exercises" (*fechtübungen*), and those that belong to the exercise areas of Educational Gymnastics...

§. 5. Although the exercises with fencing weapons do not belong to the Educational Gymnastic portable apparatus exercises, the cutting and thrusting weapons, as handheld apparatus, can also be used for such exercises. Namely, in that the handling of these weapons only becomes a fencing encounter when two people face each other and operate against each other through offensive and defensive actions, and their mutual action progresses to a real armed combat; however, the exercises with such weapons, if they are arranged and carried out in a different way than the one just indicated, can quite appropriately also be used in Educational Gymnastics as portable apparatus exercises...

§. 7. Some of the portable apparatus exercises are very well suited to be linked to tactical and tactogymnastic movements. Where such a connection of respective movements are recommended, the leading teacher must allow them to occur as the practice progresses. In particular, there are certain exercises with sticks, flags, and clubs, which can be combined with tactical and tactogymnastic exercises in a suitable and appealing manner.

So for example, in some armies, so-called "rifle exercises" have been introduced into gymnastics, in which the bayonet-rifle is not actually used as a weapon, but is handled as a mere hand-held apparatus in such a way that certain simple limb exercises (the stretching and raising of the arms, knee-bends and stretches, etc.) are thereby intensified, and certain powers of the limbs in question are more heavily used, and thus also more quantitatively developed. For such general gymnastic purposes, however, one can also use a weapon or an appropriate piece of equipment, which one uses instead of the actual weapon operated, and uses only cuts and thrusts directed into the air very advantageously...

In the remainder of his 1862 text, Rothstein largely presents a greatly condensed, simplified version of his 1855 club exercises (containing new, but fewer, illustrations), all of which are to be performed with a non-martial, calisthenic mindset—that is, within the explicit confines of Educational Gymnastics. This alteration from his earlier text is reflected in the mindset, selection of exercises, language, and presentation of the material. For example, in his first club treatise, Rothstein indicates the raising and lowering of the club by the commands: *"Wehr auf!"* and *"Wehr ab!"*, which roughly translate to: "Raise arms!" and "Lower arms!", in the military sense. However, in his later 1862 text, Rothstein replaces these commands with *"Keule auf!"* and *"Keule ab!"* (which roughly translate to "Raise club!" and "Lower club!"), thus consciously divesting these commands of their original martial character. However, it is important to note that the 1862 text is not merely an abridged rehash of the same techniques, but includes three new exercises, mainly for the cultivation of arm and upper body strength.[60] Two of the three new exercises bear a more than passing resemblance to club exercises published during the earlier part of the century by Amorós, whose treatise (as

---

60 Rothstein, *Die Geräth-Uebungen.*

previously recounted) Rothstein had reviewed.[61] Although Rothstein had found those exercises to not be "praiseworthy and recommendable" at the time, he had evidently experienced a change of heart, or had liked two of them well enough to include in his new syllabus.

We have already detailed how Rothstein treated of the club within the branches of both Military and Educational Gymnastics. As it turns out, Rothstein utilized the club in a third branch as well: that of Aesthetic Gymnastics. In contrast to the others, the objective of this branch was self-expression, and included more artistic, dance-like movements, as well as "mime-like forms" in which the gymnasts interpreted characters, scenes, and dynamic physical positions from history, literature, and mythology. Ling was unable to complete this branch during his lifetime, and left its further development to his disciples.

In 1865, a book containing Rothstein's illustrations of Aesthetic Gymnastics was published posthumously in his hometown of Erfurt. The positions illustrated in this book were inspired by a variety of sources, including classical mythology, ancient Greek and Roman history, Shakespearean drama, and, most importantly, Ling's own epic poems which were themselves based on Scandinavian legend.[62] Early in his career, Ling had acquainted himself with Sweden's history and legendary past, and became deeply involved in Nordic mythology. As a co-founder of the Gothic association (*Götiska Förbundet*) in 1811, he was devoted to developing a particular Swedish nationalism out of a romantic past, against the background of the Swedish new constitution of 1809, and against the loss of Finland that same year. Ling's goal was to present all of Swedish history in epic, lyric, and dramatic works.[63] He wrote a number of epic poems, including the eight-hundred page *Asarne,* which tells a fantastic story based on Swedish legend. Among the incidents it describes are numerous battles and single combats with large clubs.[64] Rothstein illustrates one such scene from this text, as the basis for a physical position in his treatment of Aesthetic Gymnastics (see Fig. 40).

Knowing all of this, the modern reader might well wonder: was Rothstein's method ultimately more German, or Swedish? The answer is not

61 Amoros, Plate XXI.
62 Hugo Rothstein, *Aus Hugo Rothsteins Nachlass für seine Freunde* (Erfurt: 1865).
63 *The Nordic Journal of Educational History*, Vol. 4, no. 2 (2017): 5.
64 Pehr Henrik Ling, *Asarne* (Stockholm: L. J. Hjerta, 1833), 70-76, 98, 129-30, 224-26, 251, 412-13, 537, 553-54, 571, 655.

Fig. 40. Aesthetic Gymnastics with the club, according to Rothstein. Plate XXI from Aus Hugo Rothsteins Nachlass für seine Freunde, *Erfurt, 1865.*

so clear. It is recorded that while Rothstein was in Stockholm, he learned both fencing and gymnastics.[65] And Ling's fencing curriculum certainly encompassed a variety of weapons, both long and short, both one-handed and two-handed, both heavy and light. By way of example, Rothstein mentions in his treatment of the pike or spear (*spieß*), as part of his much larger work, *Die Wehrgymnastik,* that his knowledge of that weapon comes directly from the Ling method, down to exact weapon specifications.[66] Therefore, it is certainly possible that Rothstein learned a specific club-fencing exercise at the Central Institute as part of his training in

---

65 Rothstein, *Die Königliche*, 2.
66 Rothstein, *Wehrgymnastik*, 198.

military gymnastics, and that this is exactly what he presents in his 1855 text. As one German author speculated: "I do not know where Rothstein got to learn the use of the clubs, but with that admirer of foreign character one can certainly assume foreign origin."[67] Yet another possibility is that, as the student of a holistic and comprehensive fencing method, Rothstein simply applied his knowledge of fencing theory to an unfamiliar weapon—the club—in order to offer something useful and unique at his Berlin Institute. Still another possibility is that Rothstein learned pre-existing techniques and then blended or modified them himself. Unfortunately, Rothstein does not inform the reader as to the explicit origins of his method. However, even in the event that Rothstein alone devised it, it must be said that his method was certainly not created out of thin air, isolated in a technical bubble, but is reflective of the Swedish fencing theory which was very much alive during his time.

Whatever the case, Rothstein certainly seems to have had his own ideas, which he added to what he had already learned. According to a later Turner handbook:

Rothstein not only used Ling's printed writings for his published works, but used also the unpublished notes that Ling left behind. His main work, however, is based on his own reflections and very detailed additional studies, so that it is quite justified if one speaks of *Ling-Rothsteinscher* gymnastics in Germany. Rothstein not only expanded Ling-gymnastics, but he also philosophically justified it.[68]

Or, as another defender of Rothstein declared even more forcefully:

Even if the Swede, Ling, is to be regarded as the founder of that system, the main representative and editor of it, Major Rothstein of Berlin, has taken such an important part in the development and completion of this system, especially the branches of Educational and Military Gymnastics, that in view of the rare piety that Rothstein shows in all his writings towards Ling, it can only appear to be a demand of justice if the wish is here expressed to call this system in Germany in the future Rothstein's System of Gymnastics...we believe that we have all the more reason to set up his name as the authoritative one for [these] branches of gymnastics...[69]

---

67 Wortmann (1905), 17.
68 Rudolf Gasch, *Handbuch des gesamten Turnwesens und der verwandten Leibesübungen* (Wien & Leipzig: Pichler, 1920), 557.
69 Hermann Kaiser, *Das Rothstein'sche System der Gymnastik in seiner Stellung zur*

In the end, its general uniqueness aside, perhaps the most striking aspect of Rothstein's treatise is his focus and insistence on proper form and aesthetics. Rothstein took a blunt, heavy weapon that was popularly regarded as one of the most primitive and barbaric in the history of mankind, and presents a method for its use which is martial in nature, but intended to develop perfection of form, precision of movement and positioning, and aesthetic beauty. Though this may come as a surprise to the modern reader, who might even regard this mindset with strangeness or confusion, it is very much in keeping with the philosophy of traditional Swedish gymnastics, which emphasized form and "the quality of the movements" above all else.[70] As one prominent disciple of Ling's method explained, "good form in execution usually decides the extent of the effect."[71] Or, in the words of Hugo Rothstein himself: "The weapon must not rule the fencer; the fencer must rule the weapon."[72]

Deutschen Turnkunst: Ein Wort zur Verständigung an alle Freunde geordneter Leibesübungen (Berlin: E. H. Schröder, 1861), 8-9.

70 Ling, *Gymnastikens allmänna grunder,* 195.

71 Baron Nils Posse, *The Special Kinesiology of Educational Gymnastics,* 5.

72 Rothstein, *Wehrgymnastik,* 198.

Fig. 41. Hugo Rothstein (1810-1865). From Ruhl's Deutsche Turner
in Wort und Bild, *Leipzig and Vienna, 1901.*

III.

THE METHOD OF HANDLING THE CLUB AS A GYMNASTIC EXERCISE.

by

Hg. Rothstein.

In its proper sense, the use of the club belongs to Military Gymnastics. In my systematic presentation of the latter[*], I have shown in §2 in more detail into which special areas it is divided; namely, apart from the throwing exercises, insofar as these are arranged and practiced for the combat with missile weapons, military gymnastics arises in the wrestling-fight and in the combat with weapons, i. e., in wrestling and fencing, its two main areas. This division was derived in principle from the fact that the fight between human individuals is carried out either solely and directly with one's own limbs, or that one makes use of external means (weapons), and the shape and characteristics of the weapons are essential factors that determine the positions and movements.

---

[*] Hugo Rothstein, *Die Gymnastik nach P. H. Lings System. Abschnitt IV. Die Wehrgymnastik*. Berlin, 1851.

It has now also been shown with regard to armed combat why, when considered as gymnastics, it excludes the use of firearms, and why the only weapons that are used in gymnastic combat are those that are governed and moved directly and solely by the combatant's own physical powers and whose effect, apart from the element of gravity (which affects all bodies), solely results from those bodily powers. In other words: gymnastic armed combat includes only the fight with the so-called thrusting and cutting weapons. —

The other restrictions for the well-ordered execution of the armed combat, or the fencing exercises, that still have to be observed in the selection of the weapons to be used is also stated in §2 of the aforemen-tioned systemic presentation, and I content myself here to briefly remark that there, only the customary thrusting and cutting weapons (smallsword, bayonet-rifle and spear, lance, saber and *pallasch*) were addressed, and the use of these was explained in more detail, in that the art of fencing as a branch of military gymnastics and as an art of a regu-lated armed combat cannot properly deal with creating specific instruc-tions for each and every conceivable kind of weapon. It was also stated that at least the use of items that are of a more or less regular shape and especially suitable for fighting can be derived from the artful use of the weapons mentioned above.

The club is obviously one such item, of which it must be said, that its method of combative use could actually be made the object of gymnastic exercise, and from which the aforementioned systematic presentation of military gymnastics was only abstracted, because the club is no longer considered one of our national weapons. It can be added that the omis-sion of the use of the club in that depiction was probably all the more justified, as the exercises in it cannot be continued up to the point of free fencing assaults, and a realistic fight with clubs cannot be carried out by the practitioners; because even the strongest means of protection commonly used in other free-fencing exercises (strong fencing masks[73], breastplates, strong long gloves, etc.) would not adequately protect the

---

73 "Fencing masks in the proper sense were still not ubiquitous in the German states at that point in time. A type of hat with a rather wide brim that would fold over and protect the face during a cut, was actually still in use for cut-fencing in quite a few places, it seems. Johann Werner shows this in his *Versuch einer theoretischen Anweisung zur Fechtkunst im Hiebe (Leipzig: Hartmann, 1824)*." (Tobias Zimmer-mann)

trainees against the detrimental effects of a powerful blow or thrust with the club if it actually hit them; at any rate, in such a case, even apart from an actual injury, the severe concussive force of the club can have very detrimental consequences.

Irrespective of this, however, is that even from the point of view of military gymnastics, the mere technical or regulatory exercises in the use of the club would indeed appear to be useful, in that one would be practicing the appropriate handling of that two-handed and massive cutting[74] weapon and, in the event of an emergency, a club (or a club-like weapon), such as may be at hand, would then be able to be used with skill and safety.

But I will go into more detail about the use of the club, not just for the sake of the above-mentioned defensive purposes, but just as much, or even more so, because the exercises in the use of the club lead to a series of excellent physical movements and, in their ordered totality, can be recommended—more pedagogically than from a purely dietetic point of view—while at the same time, they contain aesthetic elements which the trained gymnast can easily make use of in a suitable way in directing these exercises. Getting such exercises up and running is all the more necessary, as, unfortunately, there are still too many worthless, and not a few downright senseless, ugly, and health-damaging exercises to be found on our exercise grounds and institutions, which every rational gymnast must feel obliged to work to eliminate.

Even if only mentioned in passing, it should not go unnoticed that the exercises in the use of the club are also recommended insofar that the exercise equipment, namely the club, can be obtained extremely cheaply and wears down from use less than most other exercise equipment. Incidentally, any practitioner can very easily make a club himself. I split an ordinary (pine) log of firewood lengthwise into two or three pieces, and cleave and carve each piece into a tapered club 3 feet long, 2¾ to 3 inches in diameter at the base end and 1¼ to 1½ inches in diameter at the end of the grip.[75] If you want to go above and beyond, coat the club with

---

74 The German word used here for cut, *hieb*, can also refer to blunt force in German (*Tobias Zimmermann*), and has no satisfactory corresponding term in English. Thus, in this translation, when we use the verb "to cut", or the noun "cut", we actually refer to a cut-like motion (as done with a broadsword or saber, and as opposed to a thrusting motion), rather than to a literal cut.

75 The old Prussian foot and inch were slightly longer than the American one (*Tobias Zimmermann*), a Prussian foot equaling 12.194 modern inches.

oil paint for even better conservation. Also check that the wood has no longitudinal cracks or splintering. — Also, don't make the club too heavy, not more than 2¾ to 3 pounds.[76]

If one really wants to engage in the academic fencing assault[77], one prepares a club for this purpose by wrapping a finger-thick stick made of bamboo or gutta-percha with tow, and then encircling the thicker part with horsehair padding; thus obtained, the body is then tightly covered with strong twine and the whole—shaped like a wooden club—is then surrounded with a covering of soft, but tough, and durable, leather.

In the following I will now supply the regulatory exercises that I set up and put into operation for instruction at the *Königliches Centralin-stitut* [Royal Central Institute], which is under my direction. — Do not progress too quickly in the course of the lessons, and ensure that the prescribed forms of posture and movement are carried out correctly and that the weapon is wielded with vigor. Furthermore, as long as the exercises are practiced as technical drills, care should be taken that the practitioner remains in the positions of the cuts for some time, even if they are executed correctly. — For the rest, you should also combine marching, running and jumping exercises with the execution of the lessons without putting your club down.

Regulatory Exercises in Club Handling.

The practitioners stand in the fundamental position[78], spaced far enough apart that the base of the club, held with arms raised and stretched to the side, touches the shoulder of the next man. If the line-up has to be done in two ranks, the trainees of the second rank stand three steps behind the front ones, in the interstices.

---

76 The old Prussian pound was slightly heavier than the modern U.S. pound (*Tobias Zimmermann*), a Prussian pound equalling 1.031 modern pounds.

77 The term used, *"freie Contraübungen"* suggests a step below "fencing assault", which is normally referred to in German sources of the same period as *contrafechten*. The fact that Rothstein feels the need to use the term *"Übungen"* (exercise) here seems to imply a stress on the non-competitive character of any free fencing with clubs. (*Tobias Zimmermann*)

78 *"in Front stehen"* refers to *Frontstellung,* a standing position of the soldier with heels together, toes out-turned (*Tobias Zimmermann*). In Rothstein's system, "the fundamental position is the ordinary perfectly upright position: the heels close, and the feet forming a right angle with each other." H. Rothstein, *The Gymnastic Free Exercises of P.H. Ling* (Boston: Ticknor, Reed & Fields, 1853), 3.

First Lesson.

BASIC POSITION, GUARD POSITION, CHANGE OF GUARD, ETC.

1. Position! — i.e., Assuming the basic position, Fig. 1.

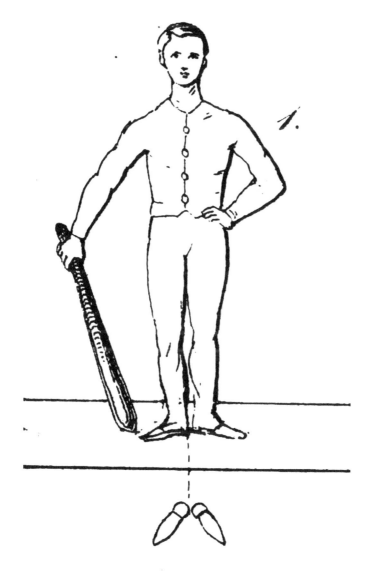

2. Raise arms! — The club, with a short swing, is brought closely past the body and onto the left shoulder, as in the position in Fig. 2; the left hand leaves the hip and grasps the club just above the right hand; the right hand releases the club and rests on the hip. — In this posture, marching and running exercises are occasionally performed. — If the basic position is to be taken up again, the command is given: Lower arms! — performed in reverse order.

3. If there is to be a change in the position of the weapon from the left shoulder to the right shoulder, this is done on: Arms right! in two *tempos*; in the first, the right hand again grasps the club, and without letting go of the left hand, pulls it vertically in front of the middle of the upper body; in the second *tempo* the left hand leaves the club, rests on the hip, and the right hand leads the club to the right shoulder. — From here on: Arms left! similarly back onto the left shoulder.

4. Right Forward Guard! — From the position of Fig. 2: the right hand grasps the club, just below the left; at the same time the right foot is placed diagonally forward by two foot lengths. Fig.3. — The knees remain straight; the weight of the body is centered between both feet.

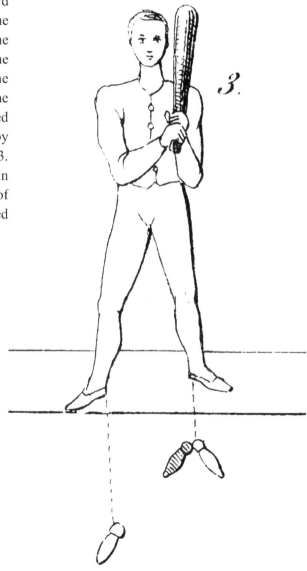

3.

5. Change Guard! — First from the right — Guard as in Fig. 3; this takes place in two *tempos*, which are now counted in the beginning, and later executed in quick succession without counting. On One! the club is brought forward perpendicular to the middle of the upper body, and at the same time, the right foot is pulled towards the left. On two! the club is placed on the right shoulder and the left foot is placed diagonally forward in Left Guard: Fig. 4.

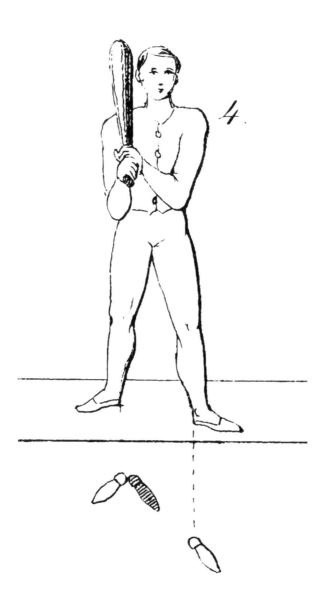

6. Left Sideward Guard! — From the guard position Fig. 3: the club is retained unchanged, but the body turns to the left by pivoting on both heels in a quarter-turn as in Fig. 5. If the previous frontal guard position is to be resumed once again from this turn, it is performed on the command: Front guard!

7. Right Sideward Guard! — From the Guard Position of Fig. 4, this is performed in the same way as described before, but with a turn to the right: Fig. 6.

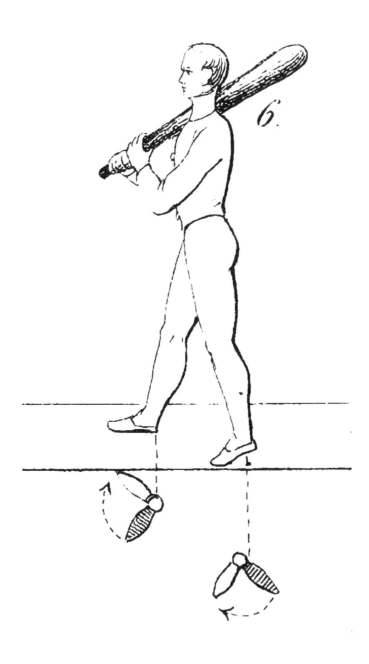

8. Right Reverse Guard! — From the Guard Position of Fig. 3: the body pivots on the left heel and swings the right leg in an about-face to the right, as in the position of Fig. 7.

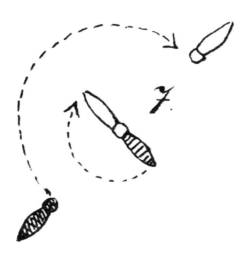

9. Left Reverse Guard! — From the Guard Position of Fig. 4: in the same manner as before, but by turning around on the right heel and swinging the left leg to the left. Fig. 8.

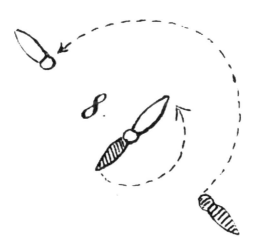

Positions no. 7, 8, 9 also become Front Guard! By resuming the guard position in the original frontal facing.

Second Lesson.

CUTS MADE WHILE IN PLACE.

The cuts with the clubs are limited to oblique *Terz* and *Quart* cuts, which may be practiced in such a way that their path forms half of a right angle [45 degrees] to the horizontal plane. — The *Terz* cut is usually hewn from the Right Guard (Fig. 3), and *Quart* from the Left Guard (Fig. 4), but in general, the first cut is from the left shoulder, the other from the right shoulder. — Both cuts are initially practiced after counting and in

two *tempos*[79], then later also without counting. The body must not sway uncertainly when the cut is executed and must not be over-whelmed by the momentum of the cut; nor must the club strike the floor. — During the commanded exercises, the trainees are to remain in the cutting position for a consider-able amount of time, at least until one can see and make sure via corrections, if neces-sary, that all have a

---

79 In his larger work on fencing, Rothstein states that every cut contains two *tempos:* the first, when drawing the weapon towards one's own body; the second, when guiding the weapon toward the adversary's body. *Die Wehrgymnastik,* 235.

completely correct position. The straightening from the cutting position to the guard position then takes place quickly and at one *tempo* on the command: Guard! —

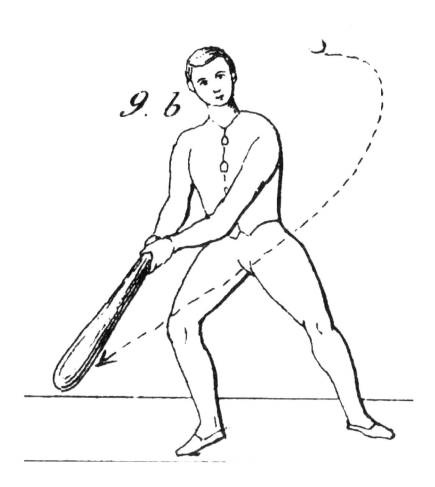

10. *Terz* — cut! From the position of Fig. 3 in two *tempos*. On One! lower the club backwards, withdrawing the weight of the body onto the rear foot and bending the rear knee (Fig. 9.a). On Two! swing the club forward for a cut from left to right down in the direction of the lead leg; the upper body inclines forward at the same time, the rear knee is stretched and the lead knee is bent (Fig. 9.b).

11. *Quart* — cut! — From Guard Position of Fig. 4: in two *tempos* analogous to the *Terz* cut, only that now the cut itself is directed downwards from right to left. Fig. 10.

12. *Terz* sideward — cut! — As in Exercise 10, only now in the first *tempo* at the same time by pivoting on both heels the body makes a quarter turn to the left, and initiates the cut in the second *tempo* on this side, Fig. 11.

13. *Quart* sideward — cut! — As in exercise 11, except that now in the first *tempo* the body makes the quarter-turn to the right, and in the second *tempo* strikes the cut on this side. Fig. 12. —

If, after such sideward cuts, in order to return to the guard position, the original frontal facing is to be taken up again, the command is: Front Guard! whereupon the practitioner straightens up directly into the Guard and then makes the turn to the earlier frontal facing. If only Guard! is commanded, the Guard position is resumed on the side to which one turned for the cut.

Third Lesson.

CUTS MADE WHILE IN MOTION.

The cuts executed while in motion arise from the fact that in the second *tempo*, i.e. at the same time as the actual cut, a foot movement occurs forward towards the adversary, or backwards, i.e. away from the adversary. — The execution of the cut, by the way, is as in exercise 10 and 11.

14. *Terz* — lunge! — The foot that is already in front of you in the guard is placed forward by a foot length in the same direction, the knee of the same leg is bent over, and the upper body is inclined forward even more than in Exercise 10. Fig. 13.a.

Quart – lunge! — Analogously as before, Fig. 13.b.

15. Forward *Terz* — cut! — The rear foot in the Guard is brought forward so that it is two foot lengths perpendicular to the other foot; immediately bending the knee of the former at the moment of placing one's foot. Fig. 14.a.

Forward *Quart* — cut! — Analogous to the previous movement. Fig. 14.b.

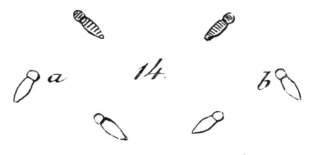

16. Backwards *Terz* — cut! — The lead food in the Guard is brought back so that it is two foot lengths behind and at a right angle to the other one; at the moment of stepping, immediately bend the knee, transfer the body weight back onto it and straighten the other knee. Fig. 15.

Backwards *Quart* — cut! — Analogous to the previous movement.

If a return to the guard position is to take place from such cuts into the original position of the feet, the command is given on 15: Backward guard! and at 16: Forward Guard! After 14, as if after 15 and 16, one does not want to return to the original position of the feet, simply: Guard! is commanded.

Fourth Lesson.

DOUBLE CUTS.

The double cuts result from the fact that the one performing the cut immediately follows the *Terz* cut with a *Quart* cut or follows the *Quart* cut with a *Terz* cut. The double cuts are also performed with feet in place or with locomotion. For practice, let them do it in place after counting, so that e.g. in *Terz* and *Quart* the *Terz* cut is executed on One! in such a way that the club is not kept fixed downwards, but is led in a steadily continuing swing to the right shoulder (Fig. 16. a), whereupon then on

Two! execute a *Quart* cut immediately to the left and downwards. — If the cuts are not executed after counting, the club does not reach the other shoulder after the first cut, but is immediately transferred into the second cut in a continuous swing, which describes a looping path in the air. Fig. 16. b.

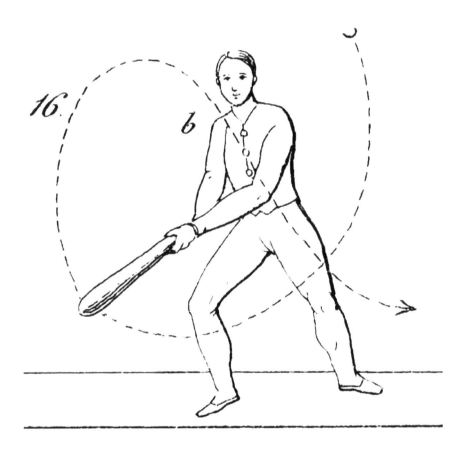

17. α. *Terz* and *Quart* — cut! — Make the cuts in place; also, with the second cut the knee of the already lead foot remains in the knee flexion as during the first cut.

β. *Quart* and *Terz* — cut! — Same as before.

18. α. *Terz* and forward *Quart* — cut! Make the *Terz* cut while in place, and the *Quart* cut with a forward movement of the rear foot as in Exercise 15; in which case, of course, the knee of the forward foot bends and that of the other foot straightens.

β. *Quart* and forward *Terz* — cut! — Make the *Quart* cut while in place, and the *Terz* cut with a forward movement of the rear foot.

19. α. Forward *Terz* and *Quart* — cut!

β. Forward *Quart* and *Terz* — cut!

Each of the two cuts is done with a forward movement, executed by the respective foot.

Other combinations, the implementation of which is easy to understand from what has already been explained, would include:

γ. *Terz* and backward *Quart* — cut!

Quart and backward *Terz* — cut!

δ. Backward *Terz* and *Quart* — cut!

Backward *Quart* and Terz — cut!

ε. *Terz* and sideward *Quart* — cut!

Etc.

Fifth Lesson.

CUTS IN CONJUNCTION WITH THRUSTS.

Although the club is essentially a cutting weapon, the cuts, at least the *Terz* cuts, can also be combined quite advantageously with thrusts, which are distinguished here as *Prim* and *Second* thrusts, by turning the right fist in the position of *Prim* during the former, and in *Second* during the latter. In order to practice [these] symmetrically, the following may be commanded:

20. With *Prim* thrust: *Terz* — cut! — The *Terz* cut is struck as in Exercise 10, but the club is immediately brought forward from the diagonally downward right-hand cutting position with a powerful upward thrust against the chest of the (imagined) adversary, so that the knuckles of the right hand face downward. Fig. 17 (the practitioner viewed from the side).

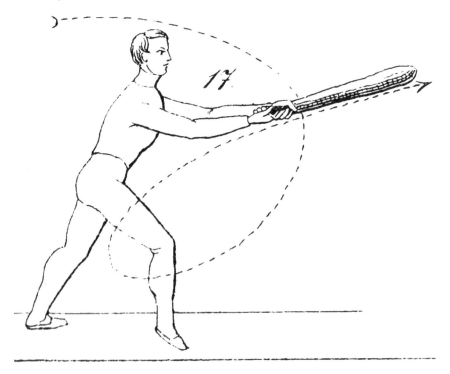

21. With *Second* thrust: *Terz* — cut! — In the moment when the club in the *Terz* cut arrives downwards, the cut is thus completed, and both fists raise the grip of the club around in a short arc, as shown in Fig: 18 (from the side), and the knuckles of the right hand come to face upward. The thrust is directed slightly diagonally downwards. —

Both exercises may also be combined with footwork: partly, so that only the cut or only the thrust, or, both the cut and the thrust, are combined with foot movements. The commands are then to be given in the same manner as in exercises 18 and 19.

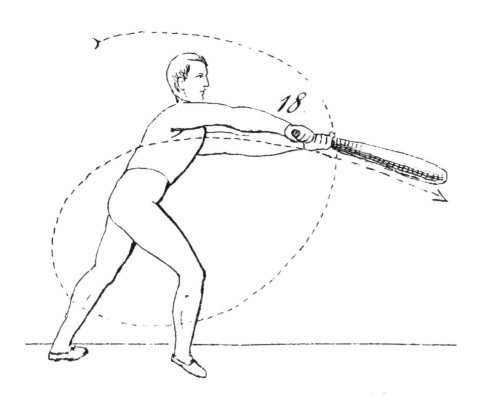

Sixth Lesson.

PARRYING, LETTING THE ATTACK PASS, ETC.

As already mentioned in the introduction, the exercises in the handling of the club cannot properly be carried out in the context of the actual fencing assault[80], so in the exercises it is out of the question to truly parry blows from an adversary that are executed with full force. However, the parries will at least be shown and practiced against imaginary cuts in accordance with the regulations, about which the following should now be noted:

22. The parrying of club cuts consists in short and powerful counter-cuts; merely passively catching the massive incoming blow would be entirely inadequate. — The *Terz* cut is parried with a *Terz* counter-cut, the *Quart* cut with a *Quart* counter-cut, the adversary's blow being caught by your own club on the part of it where its center of gravity lies.

If the practitioners do not face each other during the exercises, the command is: *Terz* (*Quart*): parry! — The respective counter-cut is now carried out with the club drawn somewhat steeply and more closely to the body, approximately according to the direction shown in Fig. 19. At the same time, the body leans back a little and sinks onto the bent rear knee.

If the practitioners stand facing each other in measure[81], only the attacker's cut would be commanded, and the defender would then have to execute the respective counter-cut.

---

80 The fencing assault (*contrafechten*), according to Rothstein, "represents the course of a realistic one-on-one combat, in which, only for the sake of avoiding bodily injury, the necessary means of protection (fencing masks, etc.) must not be left unused." *Die Wehrgymnastik*, 126.

81 Measure (*mensur*): "If two fencers ready to fence face one another in such a way that at any moment the attack can take place immediately [with a lunge], i.e., the distance between the two fencers is called the measure." *Die Wehrgymnastik*, 86.

23. Most of the time you will do well to combine the parry with a backwards movement of the lead foot (similar to exercise 16), and this is to be practiced on the command: backwards *Terz* (*Quart*): parry!

24. In addition, however, it is also often used with great advantage to "let the attack pass", whereby one completely avoids the adversary's cut by a suitable backward movement or sidestep without making a counter-cut.

25. When "letting the attack pass", one must not stop at mere dodging, but immediately after the adversary's cut has missed its mark, carry out a riposte by cut or by thrust with a rapid forward movement.

Incidentally, a riposte by cut or by thrust by the person parrying will often be possible, if the adversary's cut has been parried by a counter-cut.

"Letting the attack pass" and the riposte by cut are not specifically commanded by the teacher, but only announced in general [beforehand].

26. Finally, one may practice "letting the attack pass", with which one behaves purely defensively and respectively retreats from his adversary. After having practiced this defense in place, have it performed on the command: backward swinging defense: defend! This defense takes place approximately in the form of continuous double cuts, by guiding the club in a looping path and making a continuous backward movement (similar to exercise 16) with the feet.

—

Once the instructor has become properly acquainted with the regulatory forms given above and the students have gained confidence and skill in them, it is easy to combine the various forms, on the basis of certain suppositions, in such a way that at least a simulated combat with clubs can be performed. — If the individual regulatory forms of club-handling show themselves to be aesthetic elements, both in the movements and by being retained as positions, they can be combined even more sensibly into club combat, especially as such the addition of other positions and movements not only allow, but even demand according to the necessary suppositions, to be arranged and carried out in one overall measure as an aesthetic representation. But don't rush to get to this point!

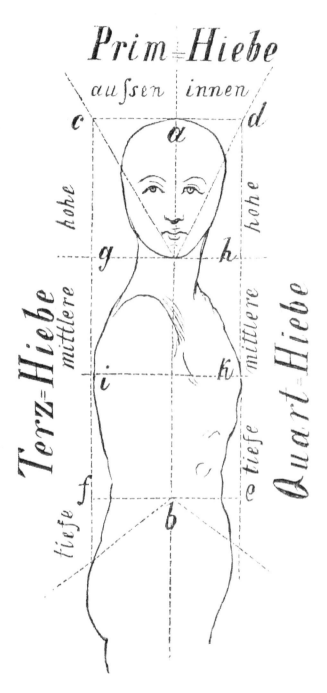

Fig. 42. Rothstein's diagram for Hiebfechten (cut-fencing), applied to the saber, in his Das Stoss- und Hiebfechten mit Degen und Säbel, Berlin, 1863.

Full original plate from Rothstein's Die Keulenführung als Gymnastische Uebung.

IV.

DIE KEULENFÜHRUNG ALS GYMNASTISCHE UEBUNG.

Von

HG. ROTHSTEIN.

D ie Keulenführung gehört ihrer eigentlichen Bedeutung nach der Wehrgymnastik an. In meiner systematischen Darstellung der Letztern[*] habe ich im § 2 näher nachgewiesen, in welche besondere Gebiete sich dieselbe theilt; nämlich abgesehen von den Wurfübungen, sofern man diese zum Wurfkampf anordnet und einübt, stellt sich die Wehrgymnastik in dem Ringekampf und in dem Waffenkampf, d. h. im Ringen und Fechten, als in ihren zwei Hauptgebieten dar. Diese Eintheilung wurde principiell daraus abgeleitet, dass der Kampf zwischen menschlichen Individuen entweder lediglich und unmittelbar mit den eignen Leibesgliedern durchgeführt wird, oder dass man sich dabei

---

[*] „Hg. Rothstein, *die Gymnastik nach P. H. Lings System. Abschnitt IV. die Wehrgymnastik*. Berlin 1851.“

äusserer Mittel, der Waffen, bedient, und die Einrichtung und Beschaf fenheit der Waffen die Stellungen und Bewegungen wesentlich mit bedingt.

Es wurde nun ferner in Betreff des Waffenkampfs nachgewiesen, weswegen er als gymnastischer die Anwendung der Schiesswaffen aussschliesst und im gymnastischen Kampfe nur solche Waffen in Anwendung kommen, welche unmittelbar und allein durch des Kämpfenden eigne Leibeskraft regiert und bewegt werden und deren Wirkung, abgesehen von der allen Körpern zukommenden Schwerkraft, einzig aus jener Leibeskraft resultirt. Mit andern Worten: der gymnastische Waffenkampf umfasst nur das Gefecht mit den s. g. Stossund Hiebwaffen. – .

Welche andere Beschränkungen für die wohlgeordnete Durchführung des Waffenkampfs oder der Fechtübungen demnächst noch in der Auswahl der anzuwendenden Waffen einzuhalten sei, ist ebenfalls in § 2 der erwähnten system. Darstellung gesagt, und ich begnüge mich hier kurz zu bemerken, dass dort nur die landesüblichen Stoss- und Hiebwaffen (Degen, Bajonetgewehr und Spiess, Lanze, Säbel und Pallasch) angenommen und die Führung derselben näher dargelegt wurde, indem die Fechtkunst als Zweig der Wehrgymnastik und als Kunst eines geregelten Waffenkampfs sich nicht füglich damit befassen kann, specielle Gebrauchsanweisungen für alle erdenkbaren Waffen aufzustellen. Es wurde auch noch gesagt, dass wenigstens die Führung von einigermassen regelmässig gestalteten und für den Kampf besonders geeigneten Dingen, sich mehr oder weniger aus der kunstgerechten Gebrauchsweise der vorhin genannten Waffen ableiten lasse.

Zu dergleichen Dingen gehört nun offenbar die Keule, von der gesagt werden muss, dass ihre Führung zum Kampfe recht eigentlich zum Gegenstand gymnastischer Uebung gemacht werden könnte und von der in der erwähnten systematischen Darstellung der Wehrgymnastik eben nur darum abstrahirt wurde, weil die Keule nicht mehr zu den landesthümlichen Waffen gehört. Es kann hinzugefügt werden, dass die Weglassung der Keulenführung in jener Darstellung wohl um so mehr gerechtfertigt war, als die Uebungen darin nicht füglich bis zum freien Contragefecht fortgeführt und ein wirklicher Keulenkampf von den Uebenden nicht ausgeführt werden kann; denn selbst die festesten zu andern Contra-Fechtübungen gebräuchlichen Schutzmittel (feste Fechthüte, Brustpanzer, starke lange Handschuhe und dergl. m.) würden die Uebenden nicht hinreichend gegen die nachtheiligen Wirkungen eines wuchtig geführten und wirklich treffenden Keulenhiebs oder Stosses sichern, jedenfalls würde in solchem Falle, auch abgesehen von einer eigentlichen Verletzung, schon die starke Erschütterung sehr nachtheilige Folgen mit sich führen können.

Ungeachtet dessen würden jedoch selbst vom wehrgymnastischen Standpunkt aus die blossen Schul- oder reglementarischen Uebungen in der Keulenführung als nützlich erscheinen müssen, indem man dadurch in einer angemessenen Handhabung der zweihändig zu führenden und wuchtigen Hiebwaffe geübt und im vorkommenden Nothfall eine Keule oder keulenartige Waffe, wie sie eben zur Hand liegt, mit Geschicklichkeit und Sicherheit zu gebrauchen im Stande sein wird.

Aber nicht blos um des oben angedeuteten Wehrzwecks willen, gehe ich im Vorliegenden näher auf die Keulenführung ein, sondern ebenso sehr oder noch mehr um deswillen, weil die Uebungen in der Keulenführung zu einer Reihe vortrefflicher Leibesbewegungen führen und sich ihrer geordneten Gesammtheit nach nicht minder in pädagogischer als in rein diätetischer Hinsicht empfehlen, während sie zugleich ästhetische Momente in sich fassen, die der gebildete Gymnast bei der Leitung dieser Uebungen leicht auf geeignete Weise verwerthen kann. Solche Uebungen zur Aufnahme zu bringen, thut um so mehr Noth, als man leider auf unsern Uebungsplätzen und Anstalten noch gar zu viele werthlose, ja nicht wenige geradezu sinnlose, hässliche und der Gesundheit schädliche Uebungen antrifft, auf deren Beseitigung jeder rationelle Gymnast hinzuwirken sich verpflichtet fühlen muss.

Wenn auch nur beiläufig erwähnt, so darf doch nicht unbemerkt bleiben, dass die Uebungen in der Keulenführung sich auch in sofern empfehlen, als das Uebungsgeräth, nämlich die Keule, sich überaus billig beschaffen lässt und sich durch den Gebrauch weniger absorbirt, als die meisten andern Uebungsgeräthe. Es kann sich übrigens jeder Uebende sehr leicht selbst eine Keule anfertigen. Ich spaltete einen gewöhnlichen dreifüssigen Brennholzkloben (Kiefernholz) der Länge nach in zwei oder drei Stücke und bearbeitete mit Beil und Messer jedes Stück zu einer konisch gestalteten Keule von 3' Länge, 2¾–3" D. M. am dicken Ende und 1¼ bis 1½" D. M. am Griff-Ende. Will man ein Uebriges thun, so streiche man, zur noch bessern Conservation, die Keule mit Oelfarbe an. Auch sehe man darauf, dass das Holz keine Längsrisse und Splitterungen hat. – Man mache die Keule ferner nicht zu schwer, nicht über 2¾–3 Pfund. – Wollte man wirklich auch freie Contraübungen durchführen, so richte man sich für diesen Zweck die Keule dadurch zu, dass man einen fingerstarken Bambus- oder aus Guttapercha angefertigten Stock mit Werg dicht umwickelt, den dickern Theil noch mit einer Rosshaarpolsterung umgiebt, den so erhaltenen Körper mit starkem Zwillich straff überzieht und nun das wie eine hölzerne Keule gestaltete Ganze noch mit einem Ueberzug von weichem, aber zähem und dauerhaftem Leder umgiebt. –

Im Nachstehenden liefere ich nun die reglementarischen Uebungen, wie selbige für den Unterricht in dem unter meiner Leitung stehenden Königlichen Centralinstitut von mir aufgestellt und in Betrieb gebracht sind. – Man schreite im Fortgang der Lektionen nicht zu rasch vor und halte auf eine recht correkte Ausführung der vorgeschriebenen Stellungs- und Bewegungsformen und auf eine kraftvolle Führung der Waffe. So lange die Uebungen als Schulübungen betrieben werden, halte man ferner darauf, dass der Uebende in den Hieblagen einige Zeit verweilt, selbst wenn dieselben ganz richtig ausgeführt sind. – Im Uebrigen verbinde man auch noch mit der Ausführung der Lektionen abwechselnd Marschir-, Lauf- und Springeübungen ohne dass dabei die Keule aus der Hand gelegt wird.

Reglementarische Uebungen in der Keulenführung.

Die Uebenden stehen in Front, mit so viel Abstand von einander, dass das dicke Ende der mit seitwärts erhobenem und gestrecktem Arme gehaltenen Keule die Schulter des Nebenmannes berührt. Muss die Aufstellung in 2 Gliedern erfolgen, so stehen die Uebenden des zweiten Gliedes 3 Schrtt. hinter den vordern in den Zwischenräumen.

Erste Lektion.

Grundstellung, Gardstellung, Gardwechsel etc.

1. Stellung! – d. h. Einnehmen der Grundstellung Fig. 1.
2. Wehr auf! – Die K. mit kurzem Schwung, nahe am Leibe vorbei in Stellung Fig. 2 auf d. l. Schulter gebracht; die 1. Hand verlässt die Hüfte und ergreift dicht über der rechten die K.; die r. Hand verlässt d. K. und setzt sich in d. Hüfte ein. – In dieser Haltung werden gelegentlich Marschir- und Laufübungen vorgenommen. – Soll die Grundstellung wieder eingenommen werden, so wird commandirt: Wehr ab! – in umgekehrter Ordnung ausgeführt.
3. Soll ein Wechsel in der Wehrhalte von der linken Schulter zur rechten eintreten, so erfolgt es auf: Wehr rechts in zwei Tempos; im ersten erfasst die r. Hand wieder d. K., und zieht diese, ohne dass die l. Hand loslässt, senkrecht vor die Mitte des Oberkörpers; im zweiten Tempo verlässt die l. Hand die K., setzt sich in die Hüfte, und die r. Hand führt die K. auf die r. Schulter. – Von hier auf: Wehr links! in ähnlicher Weise wieder auf die l. Schulter.
4. Rechts vorwärts Gard! – Aus Stellung Fig. 2: die rechte Hand ergreift die K. mit, dicht unter der linken; gleichzeitig wird der r. Fuss um 2 Fusslängen schräg vorge setzt. Fig. 3. – Die Kniee bleiben gestreckt; das Körpergewicht zwischen beide Füsse.
5. Wechselt Gard! – Zunächst aus Rechts – Gard Fig. 3; erfolgt in 2 Tempos, die nun anfangs gezählt, später ohne Zählen rasch nach einander ausgeführt werden. Auf Ein s! die K. vorziehen lothrecht vor d. Mitte des Oberkörpers und gleichzeitig den r. Fuss an den linken heranziehen. Auf Zwei! die K. auf die r. Schulter und den l. Fuss schräg vor in Links-Gard: Fig. 4.
6. Links seitwärts Gard! – Aus Gardstellung Fig. 3: die K. unverändert erhalten, den Körper aber durch Drehung auf beiden Fersen in Viertelwendung nach links gewendet Fig. 5. – Soll aus dieser Wendung wieder die Gardstellung nach der vorigen Front genommen werden, so erfolgt dies auf: Front Gard!
7. Rechts seitwärts Gard! – Aus G. St. Fig. 4, in gleicher Weise wie vorhin, nur mit Rechtswendung: Fig. 6.

8. Rechtsumkehrt Gard! – Aus G. St. Fig. 3: der Körper macht durch Drehung auf der 1. Ferse und Schwenkung des r. Beins eine Kehrtwendung rechts herum in St. Fig. 7.

9. Links um kehrt Gard! – Aus G. St. Fig. 4: in gleicher Weise wie vorhin, jedoch durch Drehung auf der r. Ferse und Schwenkung des 1. Beins nach links herum. Fig. 8.

Auch aus den Stellungen Nr. 7. 8. 9. wird auf Front Gard! die Gardstellung in die ursprüngliche Front wieder eingenommen.

Zweite Lektion.

Hiebe auf der Stelle.

Die Hiebe mit d. Keule beschränken sich auf schräge Terz- und Quarthiebe, welche bei den Uebungen so geführt werden mögen, dass ihre Bahn einen halben rechten Winkel gegen die Horizontale bildet. – Terz wird in der Regel aus Rechtsgard (Fig. 3), und Quart aus Linksgard (Fig. 4) gehauen, überhaupt aber der erstere Hieb von der linken Schulter, der andere von der rech- ten Schulter herab. – Beide Hiebe werden anfangs nach Zählen und in zwei Tempos geübt, später auch ohne Zählen. Der Körper darf bei Ausführung des Hiebes nicht in ungewisses Schwanken gerathen und vom Schwung des Hiebes nicht überwältigt werden; auch darf die Keule nicht auf dem Fussboden aufschlagen. – Bei den commandirten Uebungen lässt man die Uebenden geraume Zeit in der Hiebstellung verweilen, wenigstens so lange, bis man sieht und resp. durch Berichtigungen bewirkt hat, dass alle eine völlig correcte Stellung inne haben. Das Aufrichten aus der Hiebstellung in die Gardstellung erfolgt dann rasch und in einem Tempo auf das Commando: Gard! –

10. Terz – haut! – Aus St. Fig. 3 in zwei Tempos. Auf Ein s! Senken der K. nach hinten, Zurückziehen des Körpergewichts auf den hintern Fuss und Beugung des hintern Knies (Fig. 9. a). Auf Zwei! Schwunghaftes Vorführen der K. zum Hieb von links nach rechts abwärts bis in die Richtung des vordern Beins; der Oberkörper neigt sich dabei zugleich vor, das hintere Knie wird gestreckt und das vordere gebeugt (Fig. 9. b).

11. Quart – haut! – Aus G. St. Fig. 4: in zwei Tempos analog dem Terzhieb, nur dass jetzt der Hieb selbst von rechts nach links abwärts geführt wird. Fig. 10.

12. Terz seitwärts – haut! – Wie in Uebung 10, nur dass jetzt im ersten Tempo zugleich durch Drehung auf beiden Fersen der Körper eine Viertelwendung nach links macht und den Hieb im zweiten Tempo auf dieser Seite führt. Fig. 11.

13. Quart seitwärts – haut! – wie in Uebung 11, nur dass jetzt im ersten Tempo der Körper die Viertelwendung nach rechts macht und den Hieb im zweiten Tempo auf dieser Seite haut. Fig. 12. –

Soll nach solchen Seitwärtshieben zum Aufrichten in die Gardstellung die ursprüngliche Front wieder eingenommen werden, so wird commandirt: Front Gard! worauf sich der Uebende erst unmittelbar in Gard aufrichtet u. dann die Wendung in die frühere Front macht. – Wird blos Gard commandirt, so bleibt die G. Stell. nach der Seite hin, nach welcher hin man sich zum Hiebe wendete.

Dritte Lektion.

Hiebe von der Stelle.

Die Hiebe von der Stelle entstehen dadurch, dass im zweiten Tempo, also gleichzeitig mit der eigentlichen Hiebführung, eine Fussbewegung nach vorn auf den Gegner zu, oder nach hinten, also vom Gegner ab, erfolgt. – Die Ausführung des Hiebes übrigens wie in Uebung 10 und 11.

14. Terz – fällt aus! – Der schon in Gard vorstehende Fuss wird noch um eine Fusslänge in derselben Richtung weiter vorgesetzt, das Knie desselben stark übergebeugt und der Oberkörper noch mehr als in Uebung 10 nach vorn geneigt. Fig. 13. a.

Quart – fällt aus! – Analog wie vorhin, Fig. 13. b.

15. Vorwärts Terz – haut! – Der in Gard hinten stehende Fuss wird so weit vorgesetzt, dass er um 2 Fusslängen rechtwinkelig gegen den andern Fuss vorsteht; im Moment des Auftretens sogleich Ueberbeugen seines Knies. Fig. 14. a.

Vorwärts Quart – haut! – Analog der vorigen Bewegung. Fig. 14. b.

16. Rückwärts Terz – haut! – Der in Gard vorstehende Fuss wird so weit zurückgesetzt, dass er um zwei Fusslängen rechtwinkelig gegen den andern zurücksteht; im Moment des Auftretens sogleich Beugen seines Knies, Zurücknehmen des Körpergewichts auf ihn und Strecken des andern Knies. Fig. 15.

Rückwärts Quart – haut! – Analog der vorigen Bewegung. –

Soll das Aufrichten in die Gardstellung aus solchen Hieben in die ursprüngliche Fussstellung erfolgen, so wird bei 15 commandirt: Rückwärts Gard! und bei 16: Vorwärts Gard ! Nach 14, so wie wenn nach 15 und 16 nicht in die ursprüngliche Fussstellung zurückgegangen werden soll, wird ohne Weiteres Gard! commandirt.

Vierte Lektion.

Doppelhiebe.

Die Doppelhiebe entstehen dadurch, dass der Hauende auf den Terzhieb sogleich einen Quarthieb oder auf Diesen den Erstern folgen lässt. Die Doppelhiebe werden ebenfalls stehenden Fusses oder mit Fortbewegung ausgeführt. Zur Uebung lasse man sie erst nach Zählen ausführen auf der Stelle, so dass z. B. bei Terz und Quart auf Eins der Terzhieb so ausgeführt wird, dass die K. nicht nach unten gerichtet fest erhalten, sondern in stetig fortgesetztem Schwung bis auf die rechte Schulter geführt wird (Fig. 16. a), worauf dann auf Zweil der Quarthieb unmittelbar nach links abwärts erfolgt. – Werden die Hiebe nicht nach Zählen ausgeführt, so kommt die K. nach dem ersten Hieb nicht bis auf die andere Schulter, sondern sie wird in fortgesetztem Schwung, der in der Luft eine Schlingenbahn beschreibt, gleich in den zweiten Hieb übergeführt. Fig. 16. b.

17. α. Terz und Quart – haut! – Die Hiebe auf der Stelle; auch bleibt beim zweiten Hieb das Knie des schon vorstehenden Fusses in der Kniebeugung wie zum ersten Hieb.

ß. Quart und Terz – haut! – Analog wie vorhin.

18. α. Terz und vorwärts Quart – haut! – Der Terzhieb auf der Stelle, der Quarthieb mit Vorwärtsbewegung des hintern Fusses wie in Uebung 15; wobei sich dann natürlich das Knie des vorbewegten Fusses überbeugt und das des andern streckt.

ß. Quart und vorwärts Terz – haut! – Der Quarthieb auf der Stelle, der Terzhieb mit Vorwärtsbewegung des hintern Fusses.

19. α. Vorwärts Terz und Quart – haut! .

ß. Vorwärts Quart und Terz – haut!

Jeder der beiden Hiebe wird mit Vorwärtsbewegung des resp. Fusses ausgeführt.

Andere Combinationen, deren Ausführung nach dem schon Erläuterten leicht verständlich ist, würden u. a. noch sein:

γ. Terz und rückwärts Quart – haut!

Quart und rückwärts Terz – haut!

δ. Rückwärts Terz und Quart haut!

Rückwärts Quart und Terz – haut!

ε. Terz und seitwärts Quart – haut!

u. s. w.

Fünfte Lektion.

Hiebe in Verbindung mit Stössen.

Obwohl die Keule wesentlich Hiebwaffe ist, so lassen sich doch mit den Hieben, wenigstens den Terzhieben, recht vortheilhaft auch Stösse verbinden, welche hier als Prim- und Second-Stösse unterschieden werden, indem bei Erstern die rechte Faust wie in Primlage beim Stossfechten, bei den Andern wie in Secondlage zu liegen kommt. –

Zur gleichmässigen Einübung möge commandirt werden:

20. Mit Primstoss: Terz haut! – Es wird die Terz wie in Uebung 10 gehauen, die K. aber sogleich aus der schräg rechts abwärts gerichteten Hieblage mit kräftigem Stoss vorwarts aufwärts gegen die Brust des (gedachten) Gegners vorgeführt, so dass im Ausstoss die Knöchel der r. Hand nach unten liegen. Fig. 17 (der Uebende von der Seite gesehen).

21. Mit Secondstoss: Terz haut! – In d. Moment, wo die K. im Terzhieb nach unten kommt, der Aushieb sich also vollendet, erheben beide Fäuste den Keulengriff in kurzem Bogen herum, wie Fig: 18 (v. d. Seite) zeigt, und wobei die Knöchel der r. Hand nach oben kommen. Den Vorstoss etwas schräg abwärts gerichtet. –

Beide Uebungen mögen auch mit Fussbewegungen combinirt werden, theils indem nur der Hieb oder nur der Stoss, oder auch Hieb und Stoss mit Fussbewegung verbunden werden. Die Commandos sind dann analog denen zu Uebung 18 und 19 abzugeben.

Sechste Lektion.

Das Pariren, Verhauenlassen etc.

Wie schon in der Einleitung bemerkt, lassen sich die Uebungen in der Keulenführung nicht füglich bis zum eigentlichen Contragefecht durchführen, so dass es also bei den Uebungen nicht wohl in Frage kommen kann, wirklich mit voller Wucht ausgeführte Hiebe eines Gegenüberstehenden zu pariren. Indessen werden die Paraden wenigstens gezeigt und gegen fingirte Hiebe reglementarisch geübt werden, worüber nun Folgendes zu bemerken ist:

22. Das Pariren von Keulenhieben besteht in kurz und kräftig geführten Gegenhieben; ein blos passives Auffangen des wuchtigen Hiebes wäre ganz unzulänglich. – Der Terzhieb wird mit Terz-, der Quarthieb mit Quart-Gegenhieb parirt und dabei des Gegners Hieb mit der eigenen K. in der Gegend ihres Schwerpunkts aufgefangen. –

Stehen bei den Uebungen die Uebenden sich einander nicht gegenüber, so wird commandirt: Terz (Quart): parirt! – Der resp. Gegenhieb erfolgt nun mit etwas steil u. näher an den Körper vorbeigezogener Keule bis etwa in die Richtung wie in Fig. 19. Zugleich neigt sich der Körper etwas zurück und senkt sich in das gebeugte hintere Knie.

Stehen die Uebenden einander in Mensur gegenüber, so würde nur der Hieb für die Hauenden commandirt werden und die Parirenden hätten von selbst den resp. Gegenhieb auszuführen.

23. Meistens wird man wohl thun, die Parade mit einer Rückwärtsbewegung des vornstehenden Fusses (ähnlich Uebung 16) zu verbinden und dies auf das Commando: Rückwärts Terz (Quart): parirt! zu üben.

24. Ausserdem wird man aber auch oft mit grossem Vortheil das „Verhauen lassen" anwenden, wobei man ohne einen Gegenhieb zu thun, durch eine passende Rückwärtsbewegung oder Seitentritte dem Hiebe des Gegners ganz ausweicht.

25. Bei Anwendung des Verhauenlassens, muss man es jedoch nicht bei dem blossen Ausweichen bewenden lassen, sondern sogleich, indem des Gegners Hieb in der Luft vorbeigefahren, mit rascher Vorwärtsbewegung einen Nachhieb ausführen oder Nachstoss.

Der Nachhieb oder Stoss seitens des Parirenden wird übrigens auch dann oft auszuführen sein, wenn des Gegners Hieb erst durch einen Gegenhieb parirt wurde.

Das Verhauenlassen und der Nachhieb wird von dem Lehrer nicht besonders commandirt, sondern nur im Allgemeinen annoncirt.

26. Schliesslich möge man noch die Schwungdeckung üben, mit welcher man sich rein defensiv verhält und resp. sich von seinem Gegner zurückzieht. Nachdem man diese Deckung erst auf der Stelle eingeübt hat, lasse man sie auf das Commando: Rückwärts-Schwung deckung: deckt! ausführen. Es erfolgt diese Deckung ungefähr in der Form fortgesetzter Doppelhiebe, indem man die Keule in Schlingenbahn führt und dabei eine fortgesetzte Rückwärtsbewegung (ähnlich Uebung 16) mit den Füssen macht.

—

Hat sich der Lehrer mit dem im Vorstehenden angegebenen reglementarischen Formen gehörig vertraut gemacht und haben die Uebenden darin Sicherheit und Gewandtheit erlangt, so ist es leicht, die verschiedenen Formen, unter zu Grundelegung gewisser Suppositionen, so mit einander zu combiniren, dass wenigstens ein fingirter Keulenkampf zur Darstellung gebracht werden kann. – Zeigen sich nun schon die einzelnen reglementarischen Formen der Keulenführung, sowohl in der Aktion, als auch indem sie für sich als Attituden festgehalten werden, als ästhetische Elemente, so wird noch viel mehr ein aus

ihnen sinnig combinirter Keulenkampf, zumal ein solcher die Hinzu-
nahme noch anderer Attituden und Bewegungen nicht nur gestattet,
sondern nach den nöthigen Suppositionen sogar fordert, sich in einem
Gesammtakt als ästhetische Darstellung anordnen und durchführen
lassen. Hiermit aber übereile man sich ja nicht!!

—

Der Heldenmuth.

"Heroism." From Inbegriff der für die eidgenössische Miliz u. Landwehr nothwendigsten und vorzüglich geeignetsten militairischen Exercitien in Friedenszeiten. *Chur, 1837.*

Full original plate from Rothstein's Die Geräth-Uebungen.

V.

ADDITIONAL CLUB EXERCISES

In 1862, Rothstein published his treatise on gymnastic exercises with portable apparatus, entitled *Die Geräth-Uebungen und Spiele aus der Pädagogischen*. This book contained an abridged, highly condensed version of his 1855 club exercises, adapted for Educational Gymnastics, and intended for younger practitioners. However, Rothstein did include several completely new exercises utilizing the club. Following are those additional exercises, excerpted from the 1862 text, which did not appear in the 1855 treatise.

A. Exercises with the Club*

* A more detailed representation of the club handling can be found in the *Athenaeum for Rational Gymnastics*. Vol. II. Vol. 2.

Not intended for boys under the age of 14.

The club is easily and cheaply made from ordinary block wood with an ax and carving knife. For 14 to 16 year old boys, it should be about 30 to 32 inches long and weighing not over 2 pounds; about 2½ inches in diameter at the base end, and about 1 inch in diameter at the grip. For older and stronger trainees, the dimensions and weight are to be assumed to be correspondingly larger.

§. 10. Formal Exercise.

The practitioners line up in a single or multi-part configuration with a full arm's length distance from each other and the exercises are carried out according to commands.

...

§. 11. Elementary limb movements with the club.

The trainees line-up as in §10, but at a greater distance from each other, so that the club, when raised sidewards with the arm outstretched, remains about a hand's breadth from the shoulder of the next man. — The Exercises are carried out initially and for a longer period of time with only one club, but of course alternately (right and left), and then later, also with two clubs, one in each hand.

1. Place feet and club sideward! — Raise arm! — Lower! — On the first command, the stretched-out arm guides the club as far sideward as the position in Fig. 4 shows; at the same time, the feet assume the stride

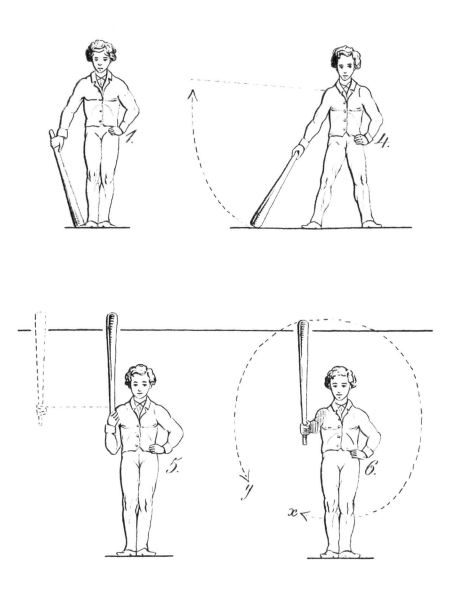

Figures 1, 4, 5, and 6 from Rothstein's Die Geräth-Uebungen und Spiele aus der Pädagogischen Gymnastik. Berlin,1862.

position. — Lift arm up! the taut arm is then raised in a slow, vigorous movement sideward to about 45 degrees above the horizontal plane; after holding this position for a while, it is then just as calmly and steadily lowered back to the starting position. — After two or three repetitions, perform the same movement with the other arm.

2. Place feet sideward, club forward! — Raise arm! — Lower! — The exercise is very similar to the previous one, except that the arm and club are held straight forward instead of sideways in the starting position, and the lift is forward and upward.

3. Raise Club! — Arm stretch sidewards! — Bend! etc. — The club is raised with a quick swing from the position in Fig. 1 in such a way that the upper arm remains close to the body, while the forearm is bent upwards so acutely that the hand touches the shoulder and the club is held upright. — On Arm stretch sidewards! the energetic sideward stretching takes place as in calisthenics. — On Bend! the club is pulled back into the previous position, and the exercise is repeated (see Fig. 5).

4. From the same starting position (Raise club), follow the same commands as in the calisthenics: Arm stretch forward! and then Stretch arm upwards! those concern the arm stretches. — With all stretching movements, the club must be maintained in its perpendicular position.

5. Hand twists. — The same are done only from the forward stretch hold, then also from the lateral stretch hold, which holds on their respective Commands are to be taken first. — From the pre-stretched position (Fig. 6), with the arm to be kept fully stretched, a steady, vigorous turn of the hand to the left takes place, in such a way that the club describes the arc towards x and then turns to the right! Returning to the initial position. Turn right! then follows the movement towards y, and from this turning back to the left. — The respective movements repeat several times; but only after the other hand has also made the same movements, the first giving the necessary relief.

Performed from the position wherein the arm is stretched sideward, the movements are completely analogous.

[*Original German*]

A. Uebungen mit der Keule*).

*) Eine ausführlichere Darstellung der Keulenführung s. im Athenaeum für rationelle Gymnastik. Bd. II. Hft. 2.

Nicht für Knaben unter 14 Jahren bestimmt.

Die Keule wird leicht und billig mit Beil und Schnitzmesser aus gewöhnlichem Klobenholz hergestellt; für 14–16 jährige Knaben etwa 30 –32 Zoll lang und nicht über 2 Pfund wiegend; am dicken Ende etwa 2½ Zoll Durchmesser, am Griffende etwa 1 Zoll Durchmesser. – Für ältere und stärkere Uebende sind die Dimensionen und das Gewicht entsprechend größer anzunehmen.

§. 10. Formelle Erercitien. – Die Uebenden treten in ein- oder mehrgliederiger Aufstellung an mit voller Armlänge Abstand von einander und die Uebungen erfolgen nach Commando.

...

§. 11. Elementare Gliedbewegungen mit der Keule. – Die Aufstellung der Uebenden wie in §. 10, jedoch mit größerem Abstand von einander, so daß die mit gestrecktem Arm seitwärts erhobene Keule noch etwa um Handbreite von der Schulterhöhe des Nebenmannes entfernt bleibt. – Die Uebungen werden anfangs und längere Zeit hindurch, natürlich aber wechselseitlich (r. u. l.), nur mit einer Keule, später jedoch auch beidseitlich mit zwei Keulen ausgeführt.

1. Füße und Keule seitwärts ftellt! – Arm hebt! – Senkt! – Auf das erste Commando wird der gestreckte Arm mit der Keule so weit seitwärts geführt, wie die Stellung Fig. 4 zeigt; gleichzeitig nehmen die Füße die Spreizstellung ein. – Auf Arm hebt! wird sodann der straffgestreckte Arm in langsamer, stetiger Bewegung seitwärts bis etwa 45° über die Horizontale emporgehoben; nach einigem Verweilen in der Hebhalte wird er dann auf Senkt! ebenso ruhig und stetig wieder in die Ausgangsstellung herabgesenkt. – Nach zwei- bis dreimaliger Wiederholung erfolgt dieselbe Bewegung mit dem anderen Arm.

2. Füße seitwärts, Keule vorwärts stellt! – Arm hebt! – Senkt! Die Uebung der vorigen ganz ähnlich, nur daß Arm und Keule zur Ausgangsstellung nicht seitwärts, sondern gerade nach vorn hin gehalten werden und die Hebung vorwärtsaufwärts erfolgt.

3. Keule hoch! – Arm seitwärts streckt! beugt! u. s. w. – Die Keule wird mit kurzem Schwung aus der Stellung Fig. 1 so emporgebracht, daß der Oberarm dicht am Leibe verbleibt, der Unterarm dagegen so weit emporgewinkelt ist, daß die Hand die Schulter berührt und die Keule lothrecht emporgehalten wird. – Auf Arm seitwärts streckt! erfolgt die energische Seitwärtsstreckung wie bei den Freiübungen. Auf Beugt! die Keule wieder in die vorige Stellung herangezogen und die Uebung wiederholt (s. Fig. 5).

4. Aus derselben Ausgangsstellung (Keule hoch) erfolgen dann ebenfalls wie in den Freiübungen auf die Commandos: Arm vorwärts streckt! und dann Arm aufwärts streckt! die betreffens den Armstreckungen. – Bei allen Streckbewegungen ist die Keule in ihrer lothrechten Stellung zu erhalten.

5. Handdrehungen. – Dieselben erfolgen erst aus Vorstreckhalte, dann auch aus Seitstreckhalte, welche Halten auf die resp. Commandes erst einzunehmen sind. – Aus Borstreckhalte (Fig. 6) erfolgt bei völlig gestreckt zu erhaltendem Arm auf linksab dreht! eine ruhige stetige Drehung der Hand so, daß die Keule den Bogen nach x hin beschireibt und dann nach rechts auf dreht! wieder in die lothrechte Stellung zurückkommt. Auf rechtsab dreht! folgt dann die Bewegung nach y hin und aus dieser zurück auf links auf dreht! – Die resp. Bewegungen einigemal wiederholen; jedodh erst nachdem auch die andere Hand dieselben Bewegungen gemacht hat, wobei die erste die nöthige Erholung findet.

Aus Seitstreckhalte erfolgen die Bewegungen ganz analog.

VI.

EPILOGUE

*R*othstein, indeed, was no ordinary man, and his memory will shine brighter and brighter. His works, which are now admired by scholars, prove that he was a scholar in every sense of the word, especially since his science was further enhanced by the finest qualities of his loving heart by a thoroughly Christian life. Rothstein, alas! has come to add one more name to the long list of martyrs of truth, who suffer here below for the cause of humanity, and whose heroic death is a thousand times more glorious than that of the greatest warriors on the field of honor. But it is not only the remarkable scientific work of Hugo Rothstein, his beautiful soul, the nobility of his feelings that will make his venerated name shine more from age to age, but what consoles us above all, because that is where the finest legacy that a man can bequeath to posterity, is that he leaves a spotless name, that he was the ideal of honour, probity and loyalty...

We who remember his activity, the inflexibility of his convictions and the sacrifice he made of himself, that he devoted himself to us, we, as well as all those who will come after us, we have as a pious heritage his works, in which his spirit survives, giving us the example of the road to follow through the difficulties which oppose the harmonic development of gymnastics.

The present cannot reward you,
Because only a few understand you;
But the future weaves laurel crowns for you,
She feels your spirit's pangs.

The truth with the flaming sword
She emerges from the dark night,
The world illuminates the transfigured one
With her sun-shield splendor.

And all see what is good and true,
That stands in unchanging being,
And evil and badness sink
To forgotten eternal torment..

And on the radiant throne of beauty
There right and truth meet
The three weave your crown,
The crown lasts forever.

   - Some Flowers on the Tomb of Hugo Rothstein
     Anvers, 1865.

BIBLIOGRAPHY

Amoros, Francisco. *Nouveau manuel complet d'éducation physique, gymnastique et morale. Atlas / par le Colonel Amoros.* Paris: Roret, 1848.

Antiquity.

Bazancourt, Baron de. *Secrets de L'Epee.* Paris: Amyot, 1876.

Benedix, Georg. *Der Turnwart. Hilfsbuch für den praktischen Übungsbetrieb.* Leipzig: Arbeiter-Turnverlag A.G.; 1921.

Burton, Richard F. *Book of the Sword.* London: Chatto & Windus, 1884.

Camann, Henry Bauer. *Indian club exercises and exhibition drills, arranged for the use of teachers and pupils in high school classes, academies, private schools, colleges, gymnasiums, normal schools, etc.*[Chicago, Ill.: 1910].

Ceuleneer Van Bouwel, Henri de. *Quelques Fleurs Sur La Tombe De Hugo Rothstein.* Anvers: Buschmann, 1865.

Depping, Guillaume. *Merveilles de la force et de l'adresse: Agilité—souplesse—dextérité.* Paris: L. Hachette et Cie, 1871.

Desbonnet, Edmond. *Les rois de la force: histoire de tous les hommes forts depuis les temps anciens jusqu'à nos jours.* Paris: Libraire Berger-Levrault, 1911.

Deutsche Turnzeitung.

Euler, K. *Encyklopädisches Handbuch des gesamten Turnwesens, B.VV.* Vienna: Verlag von A. Pichlers Witwe & Sohn, 1896.

Euler, Carl und Gebh[ard] Eckler, *Monatsschrift für das Turnwesen, mit besonderer Berücksichtigung des Schulturnens und der Gesundheitspflege, Volumes 9-10.* Berlin: R. Gaertners Verlagsbuchhandlung, 1890.

Favey, Georges. *Histoire suisse racontée à mes jeunes amis pour servir de continuation aux histoires racontées par Lamé Fleury: par un véritable ami de la jeunesse: utile si je puis.* Lausanne: Au dépot bibliographique de J. Chantrens, 1849.

Gasch, Rudolf. *Handbuch des gesamten Turnwesens und der verwandten Leibesübungen.* Wien & Leipzig: Pichler, 1920.

—. *33 Turntafeln für das Keulenschwingen.* Leipzig: Max Hesse, 1899.

Husband, Timothy. *The Wild Man: Medieval Myth and Symbolism.* New York: Metropolitan Museum of Art, 1980.

Hutton, Alfred. *Old Swordplay.* Mineola, N.Y.: Dover, 2002.

Jahrbuch des Römisch-Germanischen Zentralmuseums Mainz. 1964.

Jahresberichte über das höhere Schulwesen, Vol. 8, Jahr 1893. Berlin: R. Gaertner, 1894.

Kaiser, Hermann. *Das Rothstein'sche System der Gymnastik in seiner Stellung zur Deutschen Turnkunst: Ein Wort zur Verständigung an alle Freunde geordneter Leibesübungen.* Berlin: E. H. Schröder, 1861.

Journal Suisse.

Kal, Paulus. *Fechtbuch, gewidmet dem Pfalzgrafen Ludwig—BSB Cgm 1507.* Bayerische Staatsbibliothek, Munich.

Leonard, Fred Eugene. *A guide to the history of physical education.* Philadelphia and New York: Lea & Febiger, 1923.

dei Liberi da Premariacco, Fiore Furlan. *The Flower of Battle, Ms. Ludwig XV 13 (83.MR.183), fol. 31v.* Getty Museum, Los Angeles.

Ling, Pehr Henrik. *Asarne.* Stockholm: L. J. Hjerta, 1833.

—. *Gymnastikens allmänna grunder.* Upsala: Leffler och Sebell, 1834.

Mair, Paulus Hector. *Opus Amplissimum de Arte Athletica, MSS Dresd.C.93/C.94,* Sächsische Landesbibliothek, Dresden.

Mechanics' Magazine.

Militär-Wochenblatt.

Mind & Body.

Monstery, Col. Thomas H.. *Self-Defense for Gentleman and Ladies.* Berkeley: North Atlantic Books, 2015.

The Nordic Journal of Educational History.

Posse, Baron Nils. *The Special Kinesiology of Educational Gymnastics.* Boston: Lee and Shepard, 1894.

Ravenstein, August. *Volksturnbuch: im Sinne von Jahn, Eiselen und Spiess, und nach den in Berlin am 11. August 1861 von der Versammlung deutscher Turnlehrer angenommenen Grundsätzen.* Frankfurt a. M., J.D. Sauerländer's Verlag, 1863.

—. *Volksturnbuch: im Sinne von Jahn, Eiselen und Spiess, und nach den in Berlin am 11. August 1861 von der Versammlung deutscher Turnlehrer angenommenen Grundsätzen.* Frankfurt: a. M., J.D. Sauerländer, 1868.

Ritter von Arlow, Gustav, and Oberlieutenant Litomský, *Systematisches Lehrbuch für den. Unterricht im Säbelfechten aus der Hoch-Tierce-Auslage.* Wien und Leipzig: Wilhelm Braumüller, 1894.

Rothstein, Hugo. *Anleitung zu den Uebungen am Voltigirbock.* Berlin: E.H. Schroeder, 1854.

—. *Anleitung zum Betriebe der gymnastischen Freiübungen in den Elementar-Schulen und den unteren Klassen anderer Lehranstalten.* Berlin: E.H. Schroeder, 1861.

—. *Athenaeum für rationelle Gymnastik, Volume II.* Berlin: E.H. Schroeder, 1855.

—. *Athenaeum für rationelle Gymnastik, Volume IV.* Berlin: E. H. Schroeder, 1857.

—. *Aus Hugo Rothsteins Nachlass für seine Freunde.* Erfurt: [Publisher unknown], 1865.

—. *Das Bajonetfechten nach dem System P. H. Lings reglementarisch dargestellt.* Berlin: E.H. Schroeder, 1853.

—. *Die Barrenübungen: in zwei Abhandlungen.* Berlin: E.H. Schroeder, 1862.

—. *Gedenk-Rede auf Pehr Henrik Ling, den nordischen Gymnasiarchen und Skalden.* Berlin: E.H. Schroeder, 1861.

—. *Die Geräth-Uebungen und Spiele aus der pädagogischen Gymnastik.* Berlin: E.H. Schroeder, 1862.

—. *Die Gymnastik nach dem Systeme des schwedischen Gymnasiarchen P.H. Ling. Abschnitt IV. Die Wehrgymnastik.* Berlin: Schroeder, 1851.

—. *The Gymnastic Free Exercises of P.H. Ling.* Boston: Ticknor, Reed & Fields, 1853.

—. *Die gymnastischen Freiübungen nach dem System P.H. Lings.* Berlin: Schroeder, 1853.

—. *Die gymnastischen Rüstübungen nach P. H. Ling's System.* Berlin: E.H. Schroeder, 1855.

—. *Die Königliche Central-Turn-Anstalt zu Berlin.* Berlin: Mittler, 1862.

—. *Leitfaden zur Instruction gymnastischer Gehülsen.* Berlin: Schroeder: Kaiser, 1860.

—. *Das Stoss- und Hiebfechten mit Degen und Säbel.* Berlin: E.H. Schroeder, 1863.

Rühl, Hugo. *Deutsche Turner in Wort und Bild.* Leipzig and Vienna: A. Pichlers Witwe & Sohn, 1901.

Sandow, Eugene. *Sandow on Physical Training: a Study in the Perfect Type of the Human Form.* New York: J.S. Tait, 1894.

Spieß, Adolf. *Die Lehre der Turnkunst: Das Turnen in den Freiübungen für beide Geschlechter.* Basel: Richter, 1840.

Tacitus, *The Works of Tacitus: The Oxford Translation, Revised with Notes, Volume 2*. London: G. Bell, 1914.

Talhoffer, Hans. *Fechtbuch*. Metropolitan Museum of Art, Accession Number 26.236.

Tollin, F. *Neue Illustrirte Fechtschule*, Grimma und Leipzig: Verlags-Comptoir daselbst, 1851.

Der Turner.

Werner, Johann Adolf Ludwig. *Versuch einer theoretischen Anweisung zur Fechtkunst im Hiebe*. Leipzig: Hartmann, 1824.

Wilhelmi, Ferdinand. *Turnen und Militär-Gymnastik zu Uebungstafeln bearbeitet für Schulen, Vereine und die Armee: Gewidmet der deutschen Turnerei und Wehrhaftmachung. Mit lithographischer Abbildung einer Turnschanze*. Neustadt a. d. s.: D. Kranzbühler jun., 1861.

Wittmaack, Theodor. *Populäres Handbuch der Diätetik: oder vollständige Anweisung zur Erhaltung der Gesundheit und fortlaufenden Verjüngung des Lebens bis in das späte Alter*. Leipzig: E. Schäfer, 1858.

Wortmann, Heinrich. *Das Keulenschwingen in Wort und Bild*. Hof: Verlag von Rud. Lion, 1885.

—. *Das Keulenschwingen in Wort und Bild*. Hof a. S.: Verlag von Rudolf Lion, 1905.

Zeitschrift für Gesundheitsfürsoge und Schulgesundheitspflege, Vol. III. Hamburg & Leipzig: L. Voss., 1890.

Ziemssen, Hugo. *Handbook of General Therapeutics, Volume V*. N.Y.: William Wood, 1886.

BEN MILLER is an American filmmaker and author. He is a graduate of New York University's Tisch School of the Arts, was the winner of the Alfred P. Sloan Foundation Grant for screenwriting, and has worked for notable personages such as Martin Scorsese and Roger Corman. For the last seventeen years, Miller has studied fencing at the Martinez Academy of Arms, one of the last places in the world still teaching an authentic living tradition of classical fencing. He has served as the Academy's *chef de salle*, and has both lectured and authored articles for the Association for Historical Fencing. He is the author of *Irish Swordsmanship: Fencing and Dueling in Eighteenth Century Ireland* (Hudson Society Press, 2017), and one of the authors of *Scottish Fencing: Five 18th Century Texts on the Use of the Small-sword, Broadsword, Spadroon, Cavalry Sword, and Highland Battlefield Tactics* (Hudson Society Press, 2018), co-authored by Maestros Jared Kirby and Paul Macdonald. He is the editor of *Self-Defense for Gentlemen and Ladies: A Nineteenth-Century Treatise on Boxing, Kicking, Grappling, and Fencing with the Cane and Quarterstaff*, containing the writings of the noted duelist and fencing master, Colonel Thomas Hoyer Monstery. He wrote the foreword to the republication of Donald McBane's classic martial arts treatise, *The Expert Sword-Man's Companion: Or the True Art of Self-Defence* (New York: Jared Kirby Rare Books, 2017). He introduced, edited and annotated *King of the Swordsman* by Colonel Monstery. He has taught the German wand exercise and the use of the Germanic club at CombatCon in Las Vegas, where he has also lectured on topics relating to fencing history and physical culture. Miller's articles about fencing and martial arts history can be found on the websites *martialartsnewyork.org* and *outofthiscentury.wordpress.com*. His videos about physical culture and historical physical fitness methods can be found on his YouTube channel *Physical Culture Historians*.

WORKS BY THE SAME AUTHOR

SELF-DEFENSE FOR GENTLEMEN AND LADIES: A NINETEENTH-CENTURY TREATISE ON BOXING, KICKING, GRAPPLING, AND FENCING WITH THE CANE AND QUARTERSTAFF (2015)

IRISH SWORDSMANSHIP: FENCING AND DUELING IN EIGHTEENTH CENTURY IRELAND (2017)

(*WITH MAESTROS KIRBY & MACDONALD*)
SCOTTISH FENCING: FIVE 18TH CENTURY TEXTS ON THE USE OF THE SMALL-SWORD, BROADSWORD, SPADROON, CAVALRY SWORD, AND HIGHLAND BATTLEFIELD TACTICS (2018)

KING OF THE SWORDSMEN (2019)

.

FORTHCOMING

INTRODUCTION TO PHYSICAL CULTURE

HISTORY OF THE INDIAN CLUB

THE WAND EXERCISE

ONLINE

WWW.PATREON.COM/PHYSICALCULTUREHISTORIANS

YOUTUBE.COM/@PHYSICALCULTUREHISTORIANS

CPSIA information can be obtained
at www.ICGtesting.com
Printed in the USA
LVHW042012160123
737230LV00013B/884